P9-APO-082

Credo Canyon
Kids

Carol Reinsma

Devotional Stories for LiFE

CRC Publications
Grand Rapids, Michigan

Credo Canyon Kids, Devotional Stories for LiFE. © 1998, CRC Publications, 2850 Kalamazoo Ave. SE, Grand Rapids, MI 49560.

Library of Congress Cataloging-in-Publication Data
Reinsma, Carol, 1949-
    Credo Canyon kids / Carol Reinsma.
       p.   cm. — (Devotional stories for LiFE)
    Summary: Presents weekly devotional stories featuring the children of Credo Canyon and relating the themes of the New Testament to daily living.
    ISBN 1-56212-342-4
    1. Children—Religious life. 2. Children—Prayer-books and devotions—English. [1. Prayer books and devotions. 2. Christian life.] I. Title. II. Series.
    BV4571.2.R456 1998
    242'.62—dc21   98-5894
                                CIP
                                AC

10 9 8 7 6 5 4 3 2 1

C redo Canyon is a place where I hoped faith and friendships could grow.

My hopes were for the stories, but I found my faith also grew. Jesus was a friend who was closer than ever. I was surprised how caring people were when I asked for help with the stories—many became friends I will not forget. And my prayers grew to include those on their prayer lists.

I want to thank my prayer partners and friends Hildreth Butterfield and Barb Reinhard for faithfully praying for me. I also want to thank Ruth Vander Hart for her encouragement and prayers.

And a special thank-you to all those who helped me find stories and prayerfully cheered me on—Tamara Arnibar, Marie Champ, Amy George, Scott and Jennifer Munger, Gene Rubingh, Dick and Margaret Seinen, Margaret Jean Tuininga, Maas Vander Bilt, Susan Van Wynen, Ruth Veltkamp, John and Shirley Wind, and Joy Witte.

Next to my work area I made a small poster based on the third chapter and seventh verse of Ephesians: "I now serve the good news because God gave me his grace. His power is at work in me. I am by far the least important of all God's people. But he gave me the grace to teach about the wonderful riches that Christ gives."

Carol Reinsma

Contents

Preface 7

Map of Credo Canyon 10

Meet the Credo Canyon Kids 13

Week 1   The Birth of John the Baptist (Luke 5:17-26) 19

Week 2   The Angel's Message (Luke 1:26-38, 46-56) 25

Week 3   Jesus Is Born (Luke 2:1-20) 31

Week 4   Simeon and Anna (Luke 2:21-38) 37

Week 5   Jesus in the Temple (Luke 2:41-52) 43

Week 6   Jesus Is Baptized (Luke 3:1-22) 49

Week 7   Jesus Is Tempted (Luke 4:1-13) 55

Week 8   Jesus Calls Peter (Luke 5:1-11) 61

Week 9   Jesus Calls Matthew (Luke 5:27-32) 67

Week 10   Jesus Calls Us (Luke 6:12-19, 27-36) 73

Week 11   Jesus Heals a Man Who Can't Walk (Luke 5:17-26) 79

Week 12   Jesus Heals the Centurion's Servant (Luke 7:1-10) 85

Week 13   Jesus Heals a Sick Woman (Luke 8:43-48) .91

Week 14   Jesus Calms the Storm (Mark 4:35-41) 97

Week 15   Jesus Heals a Little Girl (Mark 5:21-24, 35-43) 103

Week 16   Jesus Turns Water into Wine (John 2:1-11) 109

Week 17   Jesus Feeds Four Thousand People (Matthew 15:29-39) 115

Week 18   Jesus Heals a Man Who Can't See (Mark 8:22-30) 121

Week 19   The Good Shepherd (Matthew 18:12-13; John 10:1-18) 127

Week 20   Jesus Blesses the Children (Mark 10:13-16) 133

Week 21   The Good Samaritan (Luke 10:25-37) 139

Week 22   Jesus and Two Sisters (Luke 10:38-42) 145

Week 23   Jesus and Zacchaeus (Luke 19:1-10) 151

Week 24   Jesus and a Thankful Man (Luke 17:11-19) 157

Week 25   Jesus and a Thankful Woman (Luke 7:36-50) 163

Week 26   The Great Parade (Matthew 21:1-17) 169

Week 27   The Footwashing (John 13:1-17) 175

Week 28   A Sad Night (Matthew 26:31-46, 69-75) 181

Week 29   Jesus Died/Jesus Lives! (Matthew 27:27-66, 28:1-10) 187

Week 30   On the Road to Emmaus (Luke 24:13-49) 193

Week 31   Thomas, the Doubter (John 20:24-31) 199

Week 32   Feed My Sheep (John 21:1-17) 205

Week 33   Jesus Goes Back to Heaven (Matthew 28:16-18; Acts 1:1-11) 211

Week 34   Wind and Fire on Pentecost (Acts 2) 217

Week 35   A Man Jumps for Joy (Acts 3:1-16) 223

Week 36   Punished for Preaching (Acts 5:12-42) 229

Week 37   Philip and the Ethiopian (Acts 8:26-39) 235

Week 38   Go Tell (Matthew 28:16-20) 241

            Devotion *extras* 247

Preface

Dear Family:

Welcome to Credo Canyon! There's a search going on in the hearts and lives of the kids of Credo Canyon. They're searching for what they believe and discovering how faith works in their lives. You may want to take the time to "meet" these children on the following few pages. As you join them, your family will have the opportunity to trace your journey of faith too.

This book is divided into thirty-eight weeks. Each week begins with a tie-in to the Bible story from Year 1 for grades 1 and 2 of the LiFE church school curriculum. Perhaps your first- or second-grade child could help you decide when to use these devotions. If you decide to use them with the whole family (and these stories certainly will appeal to most elementary school children), your first or second grader could take charge in opening the book, finding the Bible passage and the song for the week, and telling the rest of the family the Bible story at the beginning of the week. If you decide to use the book as bedtime devotions, you'll find what you need to have a special story and discussion time with your child. The time you spend together may also help establish a personal evening devotional time for your child later in life.

If your child misses a lesson or if none of your children are first- or second-grade LiFE students, read the suggested Bible story from the Scripture for the week (we suggest using the New International Reader's Version of the Bible) and then, during the rest of the week, enjoy the five Credo Canyon stories.

The introduction to each week includes a song for the week (from *Songs for LiFE,* a children's hymnal published with the LiFE curriculum) and a prayer. The song and prayer are meant to be used all week long. Each daily story is introduced by a Scripture verse from the New International Reader's Version. For most weeks the daily verses are from one portion of Scripture (although there are a few weeks when selections are made from two different books or portions of Scripture). Your child may even want to mark the verses with a colored pencil so that later you can see which verses you have read. Each day's story is followed by one or two "I wonder" statements. Wonder together about these statements and about other things that may be happening in your lives.

At Christmastime your child's church school curriculum includes the story from Matthew 2 of the wise men worshiping Jesus. There isn't a Credo Canyon story for this week. But this is an excellent time of year to explore how your family worships Jesus. You may want to use a special Christmas book or simply talk about Christmas symbols—the tree, the lights, the wreaths, the gifts, and the angels—and how these help or take away from our worship of Jesus.

Praise God for his blessings every day. Praise him for allowing us to know him through all he has given us.

Carol Reinsma

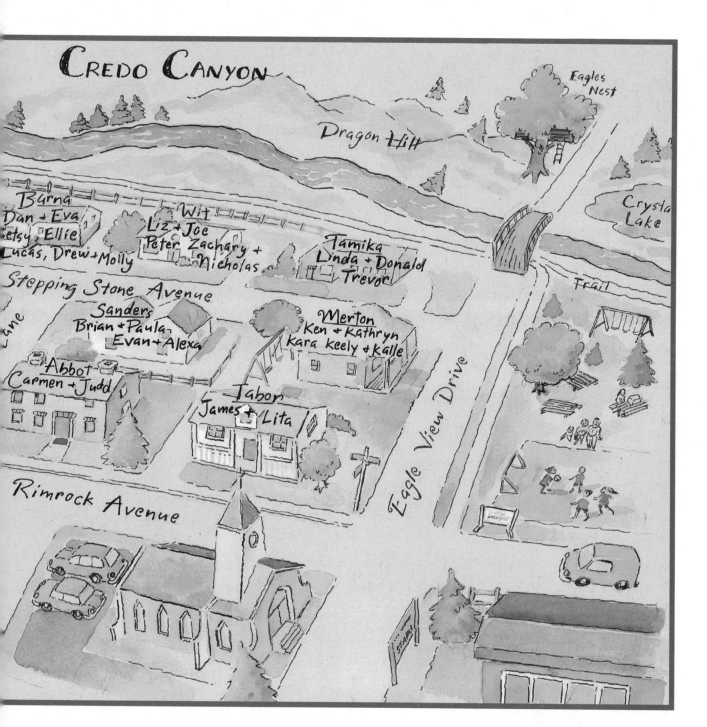

CREDO CANYON

Eagles Nest

Dragon Hill

Crystal Lake

Burna
Dan + Eva
etsy, Ellie
Lucas, Drew + Molly

Wit
Liz + Joe
Peter Zachary +
Nicholas

Tamika
Linda + Donald
Trevor

Stepping Stone Avenue

Trail

Sanders
Brian + Paula
Evan + Alexa

Merton
Ken + Kathryn
Kara keely + kalle

Abbot
Carmen + Judd

Tabor
James + Lita

Eagle View Drive

Rimrock Avenue

Meet the Credo Canyon Kids

Fourth Graders

Betsy Cochava Barna *Birthday: October 2.*
Betsy has spina bifida and uses crutches and a wheelchair. She does a good job of getting around by herself. She keeps a prayer journal to help her through the tough times. All the Barna children are adopted. Betsy is the oldest of them.

Meghan Bennett *Birthday: October 11.*
Meghan plays the piano, listens to music, and likes to write letters and ice skate. She has a zoo of forty-nine stuffed animals. Sometimes she likes to be alone, but she also enjoys adventures with her friends.

Joshua Henry *Birthday: January 17.*
Joshua is generous and caring to his friends, brother, and parents. But sometimes he wants to do things on his own. He works hard at being good, but sometimes he forgets why he is doing it. He likes baseball cards, chess, working with tools, and computer games.

Kalle Merton *Birthday: June 28.*
Kalle is full of energy and always eager to help. She collects a variety of things that might come in handy someday. She gives to others from her collections. She is good at fixing things.

Paco Ramirez *Birthday: March 23.*
Sometimes Paco acts tough. Before he came to Credo Canyon, his friends expected him to prove himself by doing the wrong things. It still can be hard for him to make the right choices.

Marisa Riley *Birthday: March 11.*
Marisa has an artistic desire to do something, but she doesn't know what. She has moved around a lot. Her father left when she was two years old. Then her mother remarried, but her stepfather left too. (The rest of her family has her stepfather's last name—Jordan.) Now her mother has a boyfriend. Marisa doesn't like him.

Alexa Sanders *Birthday: July 21.*
Alexa loves to work with paint and has won ribbons and awards for her painting. She also plays the flute and likes to jump rope and play soccer. She makes beautiful pictures, but she makes awful messes too.

Trevor Tamiko *Birthday: November 1.*
Trevor supports his friends, but sometimes he needs reassurance from them. He spends many hours designing and following Lego building designs. He thinks in pictures and is good at reading and making maps. Soccer is his favorite sport.

Peter Wit *Birthday: January 10.*
Peter is a take-charge person, and many of the other kids follow his lead. But he does not like it when others don't follow his advice. He likes to speak in front of class, write letters, work crossword puzzles, and play soccer.

Third Graders

Ellie Coman *Birthday: April 13.*
Ellie is the newest member of the Barna family. Right now she is a foster child—perhaps in the future the Barnas may adopt her. Betsy Barna helps her the most with the new adjustment, but it is difficult for Ellie, who wants to be loved but doesn't know how to be loving or love others.

Tabitha Fransico *Birthday: February 14.*
Tabitha lives with her grandmother, Carla Fransico. Tabitha's mother, Jaci, was only sixteen when Tabitha was born. When Tabitha was four months old, her mother left home, leaving Tabitha to be raised by her grandparents. Then Grandpa died when Tabitha was four years old. Tabitha loves to sing in church and tell Bible stories to the younger children.

LaReina Ramirez *Birthday: August 30.*
LaReina is the bubbly twin. Owning good things is important to her. But she is responsible in taking care of her belongings. She usually has many friends rather than just one best friend.

LeNora Ramirez *Birthday: August 30.*
LeNora is the quiet twin. Friendship is important to her; usually she has only one or two close friends. She is shy in a large group. She is loyal and dependable.

Second Graders

Timothy Bennett *Birthday: November 3.*
Timothy likes to find new ways of doing things. He's the class clown and is rarely serious. Timothy likes telling jokes and hearing new ones. He uses his camera to take funny pictures. Baseball is his favorite sport—he does take that seriously.

Janell Ingel *Birthday: July 29.*
Janell is homeschooled. Playing the violin is important to her, and she practices every day. Janell doesn't live in the Credo Canyon neighborhood, but she often visits her grandparents, the Ingels.

Zachary Wit *Birthday: May 30.*
Everyone considers Zachary their friend, and he is friends with everyone. He is very adventuresome and will try almost anything. He likes to read and go places.

First Graders

Lucas Barna *Birthday: February 9.*
Lucas is a loving person, but needs to be told often that he is loved too. School is difficult for him, but he works hard. He was adopted after his younger brother, Drew, who is always there for him.

Caleb Henry *Birthday: April 1.*
Caleb has lots of energy. He is always trying out a new magic trick and entertains others with his magic. But sometimes he prefers a pretend world to the truth.

Jennifer Jordan *Birthday: May 10.*
Jennifer's best world is imaginary. And sometimes she lives in that world all by herself. Her father left her mother after her baby sister was born. It isn't always easy for Jennifer to find the love she needs.

Huey Ramirez *Birthday: January 21.*
Huey is the reason the Ramirez family left Mexico and came to the United States. He was born two months early and needed special medical care, which his parents found in the U.S. Then, when Huey was three, the doctors discovered that he had a brain tumor. More operations led his mother to trust in God. Her prayers were answered. And moving to Credo Canyon also answered her prayers that the rest of her family would learn to trust more in God.

Kindergarteners

Drew Barna   *Birthday: August 25.*

Drew was adopted as a baby from Korea. He is a loyal helper who puts the needs of others before himself. He tries to be perfect. But sometimes Drew makes mistakes by using the wrong words or misunderstanding what is meant.

Nicholas Wit   *Birthday: December 13.*

Nicholas appreciates all that he has. He wants others to appreciate him too, and especially not to tease him. He is friendly and talkative. He gets very involved with nature activities and loves anything that is related to the jungle.

Preschoolers

Molly Barna   *Birthday: December 25.*

Most people say she bubbles with joy, but sometimes Molly is sad. Her natural mother is dying of AIDS. Molly is not HIV positive, even though her mother was sick when Molly was born. She loves to sing.

Humblelina Ramirez   *Birthday: September 16.*

Humblelina loves to sing and dance, making her the joy of her family.

More Credo Canyon People

Corey Kemp   *Birthday: October 14.*

Corey is twelve years old. He lives with his mother. His father died several years earlier, but Corey carries his dad's picture and takes it out when he needs extra courage. He is a true friend and considerate of others.

Keely Merton   *Birthday: June 23.*

Keely is thirteen years old and in the seventh grade. She is interested in fashion and decorating. She likes to improve the way things look—that works in most cases, except with her younger sister, Kalle.

Kara Merton *Birthday: June 7.*

Kara is fifteen years old and in the ninth grade. She loves animals, kids, and Evan Sanders. She understands the feelings of others.

Evan Sanders *Birthday: December 23.*

Evan is fifteen years old and in the ninth grade. He likes hockey, soccer, baseball, his dog, Buster, Kara Merton, and all kinds of shoes.

James and Lita Lenci

James is the new pastor at Credo Canyon Church. He and his wife, Lita, are expecting their first baby.

Ada and Leo Ingel

Ada and Leo are a retired couple who have lived in Credo Canyon many years. They raised their family here in a home that sits on several acres of land. They have two grown sons, one son who died, a granddaughter, Janell, a dog named Shadow, a cat named Pinecone, and several rabbits. They take an interest in all of their neighbors, but especially the kids.

Sophie TenBerg

Sophie is a retired missionary teacher. She came to Credo Canyon to live with her widowed sister, but after her sister died, Sophie kept to herself. She was lonely until she met new young friends in Credo Canyon.

The Birth of John the Baptist
Luke 5:17-26

Have you ever had to wait longer than your friends to get a new bike, a new game, or the chance to go somewhere? Wait. Wait. Wait. Soon what you're really thinking is that it'll never happen.

Because Zechariah and Elizabeth waited most of their lives for a baby, they would understand your feelings about waiting.

But what about when the waiting is over? Do you know what Zechariah and Elizabeth knew? Do you see that God never forgets his children after all?

If you are still waiting for something special, remember that God has a perfect plan. And God's plans and promises are much better than the newest thing on the block!

Song for the Week:
"Now Thank We All Our God," *Songs for LiFE* 33

Prayer for the Week:
Loving Father, you keep your promises.
Teach us to look for your goodness.
Then we will know how much you love us.

Today we want to pray for _____.
Let them know your love too.
We pray this so that your kingdom may come. Amen.

An Empty Mailbox

Trevor Tamiko wiggled the metal mailbox door. It popped open. A few thin letters lay flat against the bottom of the mailbox. There weren't any packages.

It wasn't fair. Grandpa had promised to send a treat from a Japanese store in Toronto. Trevor only had one Grandpa, and that Grandpa lived in Toronto—too far to travel to Credo Canyon for Grandparents' Day. So no one would be sitting beside him in the grandparent's chair at school tomorrow.

Trevor had planned to put Grandpa's Japanese gift on the grandparent's chair.

"Trevor," Mrs. Wit, the mother of his best friend, Peter, called to him. "Your mom had to leave for a few hours this afternoon. You're welcome to come over here. Peter's grandparents are here too."

Trevor imagined four grandparents giving Peter all kinds of presents.

"No, thanks," Trevor said. If he couldn't have a grandparent, then he didn't want to see a double set for Peter.

"Well, if you change your mind, I baked cookies."

Trevor went to his room. The Legos scattered across the room came from his grandpa. So did the model airplane and most of his clothes. One time Peter said Trevor had the best grandpa, but if he was so great, why did he forget this important day?

I Wonder . . .
I wonder if Jesus knows how sad Trevor is feeling . . .

Give thanks to the LORD.

Psalm 105:1a

Which One?

Trevor moved the curtains to the side and looked over to Peter's house. Three extra cars filled the Wit's driveway. If Peter had three sets of grandparents, the extra set could . . . he felt the grandparent invitation from school that he had stuffed into his pocket. Trevor ran next door. Deep, smooth voices and airy laughs came from inside the house. He pressed his finger against the yellowed doorbell button.

Finally Peter opened the door.

"Sounds like you're having fun," Trevor said.

"We are," Peter said. "Come in and meet everyone."

Trevor met a silver-haired man with a Grandma who had the same kind of silver hair. He shook hands with a bald Grandpa who belonged with a red-haired Grandma. The extra set turned out to be bald Grandpa's brother and his wife.

Mrs. Wit poured Trevor a glass of milk. As he drank the milk, he wondered which set was the best.

Then Trevor noticed Peter asked all the grandparents smart questions. He asked about their bones and their hearts. It was as if he knew how to take care of them. But most of all he bragged about how great they were. If Trevor had known that grandparents needed attention, he would have talked every time his mom made a call to his grandpa in Toronto.

I Wonder . . .

I wonder if you feel thankful for the people God has put in your life . . .

Tell about all of the wonderful things he [God] has done.

Psalm 105:2b

No Choices

Peter's younger brothers came into the room. Zach showed his papers to the red-headed Grandma. Nicholas snuggled against the third Grandma.

Trevor added it up. There wasn't an extra set after all.

He stood up. "I have to go now."

Trevor's mother's car wasn't in the driveway or garage. He really wasn't allowed to walk the streets after school. But he wanted to find another "grandma." Sophie TenBerg often sat at the bus stop on the corner of Thistle Lane and Rimrock Avenue. Trevor knew who she was, but he really didn't know anything about her. Probably no one asked her about her heart or her bones. He could do that.

A thumping in his chest made him want to run, so he took off full speed. He was right. Sophie sat on the bench.

Trevor ran up to her. "How are you today?"

Sophie squinted her eyes. "You're the Tamiko boy aren't you?"

"Yes, and since it's Grandparents' Day . . . I thought . . ."

"I don't have any grandchildren. However, if you were my grandson, I'd tell you to go home before it gets dark."

Trevor nodded. She was right. He waved goodbye to her.

I Wonder . . .
I wonder how Trevor felt when Sophie didn't listen to him . . .

Another Try

As Trevor neared the Ingel place, he saw Mr. Ingel outside. Soon the sun would disappear from the canyon, but it'd take just a minute or two to talk to Mr. Ingel. "Hello," he called to Mr. Ingel.

"Trevor, I'm glad to see you," Mr. Ingel said.

"I have a question," Trevor said. "Do you have grandchildren?"

"I sure do." Mr. Ingel reached into his back pocket and took out his wallet. "Her name is Janelle." He passed the picture over to Trevor. "She calls me every week. And tomorrow I'm going to her school for Grandparents' Day."

Trevor remembered a balloon that he had last week. There was a small hole in it, so the air slowly leaked out. Right now he felt like that balloon.

Mr. Ingel gently closed his wallet. "You seem sad, Trevor. What's wrong?"

"It's my Grandpa. I don't know how he feels about me. He made a promise that he didn't keep."

"I see," Mr. Ingel said. "Tell me more about your Grandpa. Is he a busy man?"

Trevor sat down and rested his head on his hand. What did he know about his grandpa? Did his bones ever hurt? Was he happy or sad?

"He gives me presents," Trevor said.

I Wonder . . .

I wonder how you can let someone know you love them when they live very far away . . .

> "In everything, do to others what you want them to do to you."
>
> *Matthew 7:12a*

A Surprise

The sun outlined the clouds in gold, then slipped away. Trevor shivered.

"Wait here a second," Mr. Ingel said. "I'm calling your mom to tell her where you are. Then I'll walk you home."

He returned with an extra long flashlight that had a wide lens.

They walked along in silence. The light from the flashlight bounced against the sidewalk.

"Lights sure make you smart," Trevor said. "They show you where to step so you won't fall."

"I agree," Mr. Ingel said.

"But I wish there was another kind of light. A light to show how to know things."

"Maybe there is that kind of light," Mr. Ingel said. "One that lets you see with your heart and mind."

Trevor thought. "That happened to me, today! I saw what it means to have a grandpa. As soon as I get home, I'm writing a letter to my grandpa."

Mrs. Tamiko met Trevor at the front door. "I picked up someone special from the airport," she said. Beside her was a short man holding a package. He had thick, white hair and bright, brown eyes that were dancing lights set in a crinkled face.

"Grandpa!"

I Wonder . . .

I wonder what will be the first thing Trevor tells Grandpa . . .

I wonder if Jesus knows how happy Trevor is feeling . . .

"Search, and you will find."

Matthew 7:7b

The Angel's Message

Luke 1:26-38, 46-56

Do you ever wonder about angels? What do they look like? What would you say or do if you saw one?

Some of you may have seen angels and not even known it. Others may have stories to tell about how angels helped you or someone you love. That's what angels do. They are helpers who work for God and you.

When the angel visited Mary, he helped by bringing her special news from God—news about how she could be a helper too. The angel told Mary that God wanted her to be the mother of a special baby. Her baby would be a Savior for all the people in the world! And Mary listened and obeyed.

Maybe you have done something that helps others love God. If so, you are acting like an angel and like Mary.

Song for the Week:
 "Song of Mary," *Songs for LiFE* 125

Prayer for the Week:
 Mighty God, you have done great things.
 I thank and praise you for sending
  Jesus, our Savior.
 I want to serve you and others in a way
  that makes
 praise go to you. Amen.

A Gift

Dear friends, let us love one another, because love comes from God.

1 John 4:7a

On Sunday afternoon Kalle Merton met Meghan Bennett, Alexa Sanders, and Betsy Barna on the porch of the Barna house. Betsy's job today was to entertain her three-year-old sister, Molly, so all the girls decided to help. They talked and rolled a tennis ball up and down Betsy's wheelchair ramp.

"I know something you don't know," Kalle said. She waited a minute, adding suspense to her secret. "Mrs. Lenci's baby is coming tomorrow."

"How can you know that?" Meghan asked.

"Before church this morning," Kalle said, "I heard Mrs. Lenci tell my mom that the doctor is going to start it."

"Start what?" Alexa asked.

"Start the birth, of course," Kalle said.

Everyone's eyes grew big.

"Then we'd better get a present ready," Betsy said. "But what do babies want?"

"Lullabies," Meghan said. "Like the one in my piano book."

Betsy hummed a lullaby song. "I can play a lullaby on my violin."

"And I could play one on my flute," Alexa said.

Kalle didn't play an instrument. She needed to find a better present for the baby. One that would prove she was more clever than her friends.

I Wonder . . .
I wonder if you ever give presents to people to make yourself look important . . .

An Attic View

While the other girls talked about lullabies, Kalle thought about stuffed animals, clickitty-clakitty rattles, roly-poly toys, and flannel-soft sleepers. But no doubt about it, Mrs. Lenci, the piano teacher and choir director, would have a lullaby-loving baby. Kalle tried to think about what she liked when she was a baby. Nothing came to mind. She couldn't even remember being a baby.

All her baby stuff was up in the attic of her house. Of course, that was it. Without saying goodbye to the others, Kalle ran home and went directly to the attic. The baby crib was stored in the east corner. A large white sheet covered the crib. She gathered the sheet in her arms and draped it over her shoulder. Tiny tooth marks on the crib railing made her wonder if she was the baby who did that, but there were no more clues.

She wrapped the sheet all the way around herself and peeked out the tiny window that looked towards the Barna house. The girls were no longer on the porch—they were probably at Meghan's house practicing lullabies.

Only Molly, Betsy's little sister, was outside. She was riding her trike down Stepping Stone Avenue. Suddenly Molly hit a bump on the sidewalk. She spilled onto the cement. Her trike crashed on top of her.

There was no one around to help Molly.

I Wonder . . .
I wonder what you would do if you were Kalle . . .

His love is made complete in us.

1 John 4:12c

An Angel

There is no fear in love.

1 John 4:18a

Kalle's foot bumped a box—'Kalle's Baby Things' was printed on the box. Just what she was looking for. But Molly. . . . Kalle ran down the attic steps, the second floor steps, out to the street, and over to Molly.

"Where does it hurt?" Kalle asked.

Molly blinked her big brown eyes. "You're an angel!"

What did Molly mean? Gently Kalle checked for bumps and scrapes.

"I'm OK," Molly said, sitting up.

Kalle helped Molly stand on her feet. Then she rolled the trike to the Barna's house.

"Since you're an angel," Molly said, walking beside Kalle, "please, visit my mama."

Because of Betsy, Kalle knew Molly's real mother was dying. The Barnas had adopted Molly so there would be someone to take care of her.

A corner of the white sheet dropped to the ground. In her hurry to help Molly, Kalle had forgotten about the sheet. So that's why Molly thought she saw an angel.

Kalle made sure Molly was safe on the Barna's porch. Then Kalle ran home before anyone else saw an "angel" dressed in a sheet.

I Wonder . . .
I wonder if there's another way Kalle was like an angel . . .

Angel News

Kalle returned to the attic. She placed the sheet back over the crib. Too bad she wasn't really an angel.

But maybe she should explain the angel thing to Molly. Kalle went to the window. Molly was still on her porch. But so were Betsy, Meghan, and Alexa. Molly was the center of attention. Kalle hurried out of the house again and over to the Barna's. Molly had gone inside by the time Kalle got there.

"Guess what, Kalle," Meghan said. "Molly says she saw an angel."

"I . . ." Kalle began.

"There might be something to it," Betsy said. "Molly has been praying for the angels to take her mother to heaven."

"That's possible," Kalle said. "But no one sees the angels."

"What about Gabriel coming to Mary?" Alexa asked.

"That was different," Kalle said. "Mary had to know for sure that baby Jesus was the Son of God."

The girls sat quietly for a few minutes.

"So what do we tell Molly?" Betsy asked.

Kalle closed her eyes for a second. "Say that the angel knows God loves her."

I Wonder . . .

I wonder if Jesus knows when you do kind things for other people . . .

How did God show his love for us? He sent his one and only Son into the world. He sent him so we could receive life through him.

1 John 4:9

The Lullaby

We love because
he loved us first.

1 John 4:19

Angels flew around in Kalle's head. She remembered the angel figures in her attic. Right now she wanted to think about angel stories and find some angel answers. Again she ran home. The door slammed behind her.

"Kalle," called her mother. "What are you doing running back and forth outside and through the house?"

"Nothing," Kalle yelled. How could she explain?

Once she was back in the attic, she found the carved, wooden nativity set. Kalle moved the figures around—just like she used to do when she was little. She lifted the angels high over the manger. The mother, Mary, sat quietly beside the manger bed of the baby Jesus.

Kalle thought about Mary's words from the Bible. Mary praised God. And thanked God for loving humble people. She gave the honor to God.

The little manger bed held the baby Jesus figure. Kalle moved the manger next to Mary. She closed her eyes to hear Mary sing a lullaby. Too bad they didn't have tape recorders back then. But she had a tape recorder. What if she'd tape the other girls while they played the lullaby? Yes, a lullaby tape would be the perfect gift for the Lenci baby!

This time Kalle knew her gift would be just right.

I Wonder . . .
I wonder if God was thinking about me and you when he sent his gift of baby Jesus . . .

Jesus Is Born

Luke 2:1-20

Do you like to watch the sunset? The colors in the sky move and change in amazing ways until the sun disappears below the horizon.

When the angels filled the sky above the shepherds, it must have been an amazing sight too. But it was more than just something awesome to look at. The angels filled the sky with praise to God. Today we use their words in many of our own Christmas songs of praise.

When Jesus comes again, his people won't be able to stop praising him either. Their joy will spill into songs of praise to God.

What about you? Can you imagine what it will be like when Jesus comes again?

Song for the Week:
"King of Kings and Lord of Lords," *Songs for LiFE* 16

Prayer for the Week:
God in highest heaven,
you brought us great joy when you sent Jesus.
Keep us rejoicing every day
so we are filled with joy for Jesus coming back to earth.
Show your way of joy to _____ .
Great is your name. Amen.

The Plan

You are God's chosen people.

Colossians 3:12a

At recess on Monday, Kalle announced her plan to Meghan, Alexa, and Betsy.

"Perfect," Alexa said. "A lullaby tape is a great idea."

Perfect. Yes, that was the way Kalle would describe everything. The Lenci's backyard met the Merton's backyard, and Kalle knew her mother would be the first one to know about the Lenci baby. So Kalle could bring the news to the other girls.

After school, Kalle was out the door with the last hum of the bell. She didn't search for pennies or any treasures on the way home. "Mom," she called. "Did Mrs. Lenci have her baby?"

Mrs. Merton hugged her youngest daughter. "It's a girl. Philida Marie."

Kalle let the new name roll over her tongue. Then she ran to get her tape recorder. "Bye Mom, see you at supper. Meghan, Betsy, Alexa, and I are taping a lullaby for Philida."

There wasn't a cloud in the blue sky. A perfect day for singing—for making a sweet lullaby.

But perfect sounds were not coming from Meghan's house. The piano and violin sounded as if they were fighting, and the flute squeaked and screeched.

As Kalle put her hand on the doorknob, she heard Meghan yell, "I can't play with either of you. Kalle'll be sorry she chose you to make the tape."

I Wonder . . .
I wonder why things don't always turn out so perfect . . .

For Philida

Everyone hushed when Kalle stepped into the living room. Alexa held her flute as if it were a useless silver-colored tube. "This lullaby is hard. I've only been playing the flute for two months."

"I think you have to play the song in a different key to match my violin," Betsy said to Meghan.

"The easiest thing to do, is just use the piano," Meghan said. She turned to Kalle. "Right?"

Kalle stared at the hole in her sneaker. She didn't look at Betsy or Alexa. "I guess. At least we'd have a lullaby for Philida."

"Philida," Betsy said. "Is that the baby's name?"

Kalle grinned. "Philida Marie. Philida means 'loving.'"

"It's a pretty name," Alexa said.

"I don't want to spoil the lullaby for Philida," Betsy said.

"Me either," Alexa said.

So Meghan sat down to play the piano. Kalle started the tape recorder. And Alexa and Betsy listened quietly.

I Wonder . . .

I wonder if you know what Colossians 3:13 means ("Put up with each other") . . .

Put up with each other.

Colossians 3:13a

Unstoppable Beat

A loud but merry voice from outside interrupted Meghan's soft lullaby.

"King of kings and Lord of lords, glory," sang the voice. Then the slap of a clap, and more singing, "Hallelujah!"

Betsy wheeled her chair to the front door. "It's Molly. She's been singing that song since yesterday."

"Fine," Meghan said. "But tell her to be quiet or go away."

"Molly," Betsy said, calling through the screen door. "You have to stop singing. We're taping Meghan's lullaby for the baby."

Molly opened the door and poked her head inside. "Poof. I stop. See, I pinch my lips together. Now it stays inside."

She settled into the big reclining chair. Her lips were pinched, but all eleven braids bounced with the movement of her head.

Then Molly spied Kalle. "You're the angel. The angel made me sing."

"I-I can explain," Kalle said.

Molly bounced off the chair and climbed onto Kalle's lap after Kalle told the whole story. "I knew you were acting like an angel. It was nice."

"She's right," Betsy said. "We don't have to be angels to do the right thing."

"If only our music was like the angels' song to the shepherds," Alexa said.

I Wonder...
I wonder if your singing praises God even if it doesn't sound like the angels'...

A Full Tape

Meghan returned to the piano. Her fingers moved across the keys without missing a note.

"Pretty," Molly said. "But no words makes me sad."

"The lullaby has words," Meghan said. "Very special words to comfort a baby. Mrs. Lenci will know the words."

"Lets us sing them," Molly said.

The girls looked at each other. Then they giggled.

Betsy reached her hand out to Molly. "You're so smart. We could sing the words while Meghan plays. Then the lullaby will be from all of us."

Meghan played the piano, and the girls sang. "All night, all day, angels watching over me, my Lord. All night, all day, angels watching over me." *

At the end of the song, Kalle said, "There's more space on this tape."

"I'd like to play a violin solo," Betsy said. So she did. And Alexa thought of a way to add her music too. She played "Twinkle, Twinkle, Little Star." It was easier for her than the lullaby.

For the last piece, Molly sang a song all by herself. Then they all whispered, "Sweet dreams, Philida."

I Wonder . . .
I wonder how many ways we can give thanks to God with our talents . . .

Songs for LiFE 199

Do everything you say or do in the name of the Lord Jesus. Always give thanks to God the Father through Christ.

Colossians 3:17

The Angels' Song

As Kalle rewound the tape to the beginning, she pictured angels as messengers, angels as guardians, and angels as singers. She pictured the angels gathering over Philida Marie. And even though it wasn't Christmas, she saw the angels singing about Jesus and watching over his manger bed.

Molly curled up in the corner of the reclining chair. She was quiet.

Kalle squeezed in beside her. "I thought you couldn't stop singing."

"I'm thinkin'," Molly said. "I never hear the angels sing."

Betsy rolled her chair over to them. "They are going to sing again—sing so we can hear them. At the very end. When Jesus comes again."

"How do you know?" Molly asked.

"It's in the Bible," Betsy said. "I have to know because there are days when I don't like having spina bifida. But then I remind myself that Jesus is coming again, and when he does, I'll have a new body. I'll sing every day with the angels."

Kalle pushed the play button on the recorder. The girls listened to their songs. They were perfect for Philida Marie.

After Kalle rewound the tape and took it out of the recorder, Meghan wrapped it in pink paper. The girls signed their names on the pink paper, and they kept singing—just because they felt like it.

I Wonder . . .
I wonder if Jesus' birth makes you want to sing praise to God . . .

Simeon and Anna

Luke 2:21-38

There's a bumper sticker that says

Know Jesus Know Peace
No Jesus No Peace

If bumper stickers had been available in Anna and Simeon's day, they would probably have chosen that one. All their lives they had prayed and waited for the promise of a Savior. When they met the baby Jesus, they knew God had kept his big promise to people. That was all they needed to know. They had peace.

What about you? Does knowing Jesus as Savior bring peace to your life?

Song for the Week:
"Song of Hope," *Songs for LiFE* 82

Prayer for the Week:
God of hope and peace,
fill my work and play with peace.
Teach me peace in your faithfulness.
Teach me peace in the gift of your Son.
Amen.

More than Birds

God is the God
who gives peace.

*1 Thessalonians
5:23a*

Sophie TenBerg hooked a ball of suet and seeds onto the balcony rail.
Two years ago she had retired from teaching in the mission school and moved to the apartment in Credo Canyon. Now she hiked the Canyon and learned the names of the birds, but there was an empty spot in her soul.

The other week the Tamiko boy had stopped her. It embarrassed her to think that she didn't know his first name or much of anything about him. If only she had taken the time to find out what he really needed. She had been too quick in telling him to go home for the sake of safety. A nudge told her that the children in Credo Canyon were her next assignment from God. She prayed for them, but her prayers felt heartless without names.

From her balcony, she watched a playground swing settle to a stop after the sound of the morning school bell. A small brown, black-headed bird landed on her railing.

Sophie held out a handful of cracked sunflower seeds. The little bird hopped onto her hand. "So little Black-Capped Chickadee, how come I know your name and not the names of the boys and girls?" The glassy dots of the bird's eyes seemed to ask her the same question.

She closed her eyes and prayed her prayer again. "Lord, show me how I can be part of your great plan to let others know of your great salvation."

I Wonder . . .
I wonder how Jesus will help Sophie find peace . . .

Free Wallpaper

Sophie opened the big chest she kept at the foot of her bed. On top of a blue silk Japanese robe was a folded piece of thin paper. She gently smoothed out the paper and read the message.

Teacher, thank you for teaching me how to read the Bible. I so surprised about Grandmother San. Miracle happened because you prayed. Love, Koto San.

Sophie smiled as she thought about long ago when she taught school in Japan—about little Koto San and how quickly she learned to read the words of the Bible.

"You may have a Bible of your own," she had told Koto San.

Koto San's eyes filled with fear. "Grandmother allows me to learn at the missionary school, but not about the religion. She doesn't know I believe." Sophie told Koto San she'd pray for Grandmother San. And she did. Even though it seemed impossible that Grandmother San could change. The priests in the temple warned the Japanese people that the Bible was the "foreign devil's terrible book."

Then one day Koto San had news. Grandmother had pasted the pages of the Bible all over the walls of their little, poor home. And she didn't know it. She had gone to the market that day to buy wallpaper. But all the paper cost too much. On her way home she found a discarded box full of paper. No one appeared to own it or want it, so Grandmother took it home. Now the words of the Bible filled her home.

I Wonder . . .
I wonder if the Bible will make a difference in Grandmother San's home . . .

May he make you holy through and through.

1 Thessalonians 5:23b

The Talking Wallpaper

Sophie rejoiced that Koto San could now read the Bible at home, but what would happen when Grandmother discovered the truth of the wallpaper?

Sophie prayed for Koto San each day. And one day Koto San told her a wonderful story.

Koto San explained that every day as she sat close to the wall reading the Bible, she grew braver. One day she said, "Grandmother—sometimes as I sit here drinking tea, the wallpaper talks to me!"

Grandmother thought Koto San was being silly, but Koto San insisted it was true.

So Grandmother asked Koto San what the wallpaper said.

Koto San told about the great God in heaven who made the sun, moon, and stars.

Every day Koto San read more pages to Grandmother. She read about Adam and Eve who listened to Satan and disobeyed God.

"Ai yah!" Grandmother said. "Ai yah! How sad! Does the wallpaper say God punished them?"

Koto nodded. "They had to die."

"My heart is wicked too," Grandmother said. "Must God punish me?"

"Not if you believe the best story of all. God sent a Savior—God's own Son. He came from the highest heaven to earth to bring forgiveness. But he had to die to pay for it." "Savior." Grandmother whispered the beautiful word.

I Wonder . . .
I wonder if you think "Savior" is a beautiful word . . .

May you be without blame from now until our Lord Jesus Christ comes.

1 Thessalonians 5:23c

The Wallpaper of Truth

One morning after Koto San left for school, Grandmother dressed in her best kimono. She hurried to the priest to ask about the wonderful stories from the wallpaper.

As soon as Grandmother San told the priest about Jesus Christ, the priest became angry. He accused Grandmother of listening to the evil book. He slammed the door in Grandmother's face. Her tears spilled onto the dusty road.

But she did not give up. She went back to the yard where she found the box of paper. When she knocked on the door of the house, a woman with straw-colored hair answered the door. Grandmother forgot her manners and stared. However, the woman invited Grandmother into the house, and Grandmother poured out her story.

"Tell me, is it true?" Grandmother asked. "Does God really love me?"

"God does!" said the woman. "And whoever believes in Jesus will live forever."

Grandmother fell down on her knees. She wept and thanked God for loving a poor old Japanese woman. Then she quickly rose to her feet, thanked the missionary for her help, and hurried home.

When Koto San got home, Grandmother met her at the door.

"Oh, Koto San! What do you think I found out today? Our wallpaper is really the Bible!"

Koto San was frightened until she saw the joy on Grandmother's face.

I Wonder . . .

I wonder how many amazing and unusual ways our great God uses to teach people about love . . .

I wonder what stories you can tell about God's faithfulness to you . . .

The One who has chosen you is faithful.

1 Thessalonians 5:24a

Prayers in the Canyon

What a difference prayer made, Sophie thought as she folded Koto San's letter and put it back in the chest.

With the chest of yesterday's memories closed, Sophie knew it was time to move forward in a new direction—different from her quiet life in Credo Canyon.

It was hard to change, but with God anything was possible. After all, God changed the world by sending a baby. A butterfly feeling dusted her heart.

There was a new baby in Credo Canyon—baby Philida Marie—the first child of the young preacher and his wife. Sophie could start by being a part of this baby's life.

Using special pens and ink, she wrote a prayer for the baby on delicate rice paper. She folded the paper, put it into a matching envelope, and left her apartment.

As Sophie approached the Lenci house, she heard giggling voices. Through the window she could see that the girls from the neighborhood were visiting too.

Sophie knocked on the door, and Mrs. Lenci invited her to join the others and sit down to hold the baby. As Sophie rocked the baby in her arms, she listened to the girls talk about school and all their activities. Soon she learned their names and the names of the boys in their school too. She could tell that they enjoyed special activities. Perhaps they'd have fun at a Japanese-style tea party after school. Yes, that's what she'd do. It'd be a time to listen and a time to know how to pray for the girls and boys in Credo Canyon.

I Wonder...
I wonder what kind of peace Sophie will have as she prays for the Credo Canyon kids . . .

He will give perfect peace to those who commit themselves to be faithful to him.

Isaiah 26:3

Jesus in the Temple
Luke 2:41-52

Has anyone ever told you that you laugh like your dad? Or talk like your mom? People in the same family often do similar things.

When Jesus was a twelve-year-old boy, he answered the questions from the teachers in the temple. His answers were so wise that it was obvious he was like his heavenly Father. But Jesus was like us too. So he knows what we need. He also invites us to be in his family with God.

Once you belong to him, you'll want to be like him.

Song for the Week:
"May the Mind of Christ, My Savior," *Songs for LiFE* 72

Prayer for the Week:
Jesus, you are the Son of God.
But you were a child too.
That tells me you know God's way
and my ways.
Thank you for coming to earth
to be like us so you could tell us about God.
Now teach us how to be like you. Amen.

The Birthday Box

Five o'clock. Corey Kemp's alarm clock started its familiar call. With his eyes closed, he reached over to quiet the deep-beep, deep-beep. Automatically he rolled out of his blanket nest and onto the floor.

Ever since his dad died, his mom worked an early shift at the nursing home. So every workday, he crawled out of bed to join her for breakfast.

Somewhere between his bed and the breakfast table he woke up. A steaming platter of French toast sat beside a large, square box covered with birthday paper. Now Corey was definitely awake. Yes, today was his twelfth birthday. The box was bigger than necessary for a pair of running shoes. But sometimes . . .

"Before you open your present," Jeanne Kemp said, "there is something you should know. This isn't a present from the store. It's from your father. Before he died he asked me to put these things in a box and give them to you on your twelfth birthday."

Corey touched the blue, papered box as if it might disappear.

Jeanne Kemp placed her hand on Corey's shoulder. "Go ahead. Open it. Your father said these were the two most important things to him when he was twelve."

Corey's heart pounded in his ears as he tore away the paper. An old pair of sneakers—worn and grungy, and a dark, brown leather-covered Bible sat inside the box.

I Wonder . . .
I wonder if Corey's father's things will be important to Corey . . .

> We have been asking God to fill you with the knowledge of what he wants.
>
> *Colossians 1:9b*

Discovery

Corey rubbed the smooth bottom of a sneaker against his cheek. "There's not any tread left on these shoes."

His mom poked at the other shoe. "At the end of the week, when I get paid, we can buy the new running shoes you wanted."

Corey swallowed against the cotton ball in his throat. "Thanks. Was Dad a runner the same as I am?"

"I think that's one thing he wanted you to know about him. Between the pages of the Bible there's more of his story."

Corey picked up the Bible. It seemed plain compared to his Bible with its flashy cover and study notes. As his thumb slid over the page edges, he noticed that the Bible was stuffed with snapshots, notecards, and scraps of paper. Were these clues about the father that he didn't remember?

Jeanne Kemp turned her arm to look at her watch. "I have to go now, Corey. Will you be okay?"

Corey nodded. He was more than okay. He felt a newness rush through him. It was almost as if his father were reaching down to him—telling him things he wanted to know about being his father's son.

I Wonder . . .

I wonder what Corey can learn about his father from the words and pictures that were in his Bible . . .

We want you to grow to know God better.

Colossians 1:10b

A Dog Clue

Corey flipped the Bible so that the pages fanned downward. Several pictures slipped into his lap. He studied the boys' faces in one picture—no one he recognized. The next picture was of a dog. This time he sensed something familiar in the dog's coloring and face.

His thoughts concentrated on the dog as he cleaned up breakfast dishes. Shadow! Mr. Ingel's dog had the same markings—a black lab—as black as midnight, with a small white streak running up its nose.

Shadow was old. Corey never saw him run after a ball. Old Shadow just yawned and stretched out under the warm sun. But if Shadow had belonged to his dad, then why did Mr. Ingel have him?

With a sinking feeling Corey remembered the rules of the apartment building. No Pets. But couldn't his mother have done something if she really wanted him to know a part of his father? There were too many unfair things in his life. Why did he have to wait this long to find out about his dad's dog? Things could have been different if Shadow had been his dog.

The chores would have to wait. Corey ran out of the apartment building and cut across the field and the corner by the school to the Ingel's house.

I Wonder . . .
I wonder how many other questions Corey has about his dad . . .

We want you to be very strong, in keeping with his glorious power.

Colossians 1:11-12a

A Different Gift

Shadow lifted his head off the sidewalk as Corey stepped into the Ingel yard.

Corey knelt beside Shadow. "Tell me about my father. Was he a fast runner?"

Shadow tilted his head. His milky brown eyes carried an "I'm sorry" look.

"You're up bright and early this morning."

Corey jumped to his feet. He was face to face with Mr. Ingel. "I . . . I . . . came to see Shadow."

A questioning wrinkle appeared on Mr. Ingel's forehead.

Corey tried to explain, but he knew the sting in his heart and eyes more than an answer in his head. "Mom should have told me. Doesn't anyone understand? Why couldn't you tell me that Shadow was my father's dog?"

"Corey," Mr. Ingel said. "I think you've found out half-information. Shadow's mother belonged to my son, Andy. Your father and my son were best friends—they did everything together. So there is a connection to your father and Shadow, but not . . . "

Hot tears spilled down Corey's face. "Your son and my dad? Where's your son?"

"Andy travels all over the world," Mr. Ingel said. "But he usually comes home once a year with plenty of stories to tell. Next time he comes home, I'll invite you over to meet him."

Corey thanked Mr. Ingel. This was only the beginning. There must be more clues.

I Wonder . . .
I wonder if Jesus understands how Corey is feeling . . .

He has brought us into the kingdom of the Son he loves.

Colossians 1:13b

The Mystery

During school Corey doodled questions about his father in his mind and on the pages of his notebook. But what was the most important question?

After school he ran home instead of running laps around the school track. Dirty dishes sat on the counter. Torn birthday paper, the box, and the Bible were scattered across the table.

Corey decided to carefully go through the Bible page by page and not dump out anything. Each scrap of paper might be placed where it was for a reason.

He opened the cover. Stuck to the stiff lining was an envelope with his name on it. The glue from the envelope had dried out over the years, so the flap came open easily. Even though his name was at the top of the letter, Corey felt an uneasiness, as if he were opening someone else's mail.

They will know the mystery of God. That mystery is Christ.

Colossians 2:2d

Dear Corey,

It is hard to imagine that you are twelve years old. The only way I can guess what it is like for you is to think about when I was twelve. It was the most important time of my life. I've put bits and pieces from my life between the pages of this Bible. It is the only way I can think of to visit with you on this day.

It makes me sad to know I'm not going to be with you, but I know you'll be okay if you pay attention to this gift.

Love, Dad

P.S. I hope you know the story in Luke 2:7-9 about Jesus when he was twelve years old. He knew what it was like to be a boy too.

I Wonder . . .
I wonder if you know that Jesus cares very much about boys and girls . . .

Jesus Is Baptized

Luke 3:1-22

When your mom wants you to take a bath with water, it's because she wants you to be clean. You know how it works. You get in the tub or shower and scrub yourself with soap and water.

God uses water, too, to show that you need to be clean. That's what baptism is all about.

Jesus was already clean, because he was God's perfect Son. But he got right in the water anyway so John could baptize him. Jesus was baptized to show us the way to become clean. We can only be clean when we follow Jesus.

Song for the Week:
"How Great Is the Love of the Father," *Songs for LiFE* 59

Prayer for the Week:
Father in heaven, you are holy.
All your thoughts and works are holy.
By ourselves we aren't holy at all.
Forgive me for _____.
Make me think of right and pure things
    to do and say
because that is what a child of yours
    would do. Amen.

Pony?

Corey turned over the inside cover page of the Bible. The next page had a fancy border with handwritten words on the lines.

PRESENTED TO: William 'Pony' Kemp
BY: His new family in Christ
ON: His twelfth birthday and Day of Baptism

Pony? He thought his dad's name was just Bill. And why was his father baptized at the age of twelve? Corey had been baptized as a baby.

Mrs. Kemp opened the apartment door. She carried a box under her arm. "Surprise, Corey. All the people that you visit on Saturday at the nursing home collected money for your birthday. They told me to buy something special."

"My shoes! I forgot about them."

"Now that is a surprise," Mom said. "I thought that was all you thought about."

"Mom," Corey took a deep breath. "Does it make sense that Dad wasn't baptized until his twelfth birthday?"

This time Mom took a deep breath. "He didn't grow up in a Christian home. But then he started coming to church in Credo Canyon. Every Sunday and Wednesday he ran here from Mountain Shadows."

Corey tried to imagine the distance. Then he thought of the name. "Pony," whispered Corey.

I Wonder . . .
I wonder if you can tell how much Corey's father wanted to belong to God . . .

Dear friends, now we are children of God.

1 John 3:2a

The Run

Corey decided a boy who ran that far deserved to be called Pony.
Then he thought about times when he depended on God. His dad must have been like that, too, even though he didn't learn about God until he was older. That part was hard. God had always been there for Corey, even when he was little. He couldn't imagine it any other way.

Corey hugged his mom. "I'm glad you taught me about God when I was little."

"Your dad and I wanted it that way," Mom said.

"And that's why I was baptized as a baby, right?" Corey touched a tear on Mom's cheek.

"Look at us," Mom said. "A brand-new pair of shoes and we don't now how they fit."

Corey loosened the laces. "My feet were made for these shoes," he said.

"Or the other way around," his mom said.

"What if," Corey said, "I run to Mountain Shadows now? Try out my new shoes?"

Mrs. Kemp didn't answer for a minute. "Your dad made a map once. He gave it to me." She left the room and returned with a folded piece of paper.

Corey studied the map. Then he left. Once he was outside, he ran.

I Wonder . . .

I wonder if you can think of some way Corey is like his father . . .

I wonder in what ways Christ wants us to be like him . . .

But we know that when Christ appears, we will be like him.

1 John 3:2b

Mountain Shadows

After two miles, Corey had to slow down. The ache in his side interfered with his breathing. He had started off too fast. He rubbed his side while moving slowly. As the pain eased, Corey picked up his speed.

A half an hour later he recognized the small houses that were typical of Mountain Shadows. He had never walked in this neighborhood, but he had often looked at it curiously from the highway. Two bare-footed kids stared at him. Corey said hello.

"Ya have a quarter?" asked the taller of the two.

Corey dug into his pocket. He found two. He gave each boy one. Then he showed them his map pointing to his father's house—1912 High Street.

"Do you know where this is?"

The boy who asked for the quarter pointed down the street. Then he and his friend ran.

Corey walked the block searching for house numbers. He found a 1910 and a 1914— so the house in the middle had to be the one. Without paint and a cracked window, it was the most run-down house on the block. A few brown weeds grew in the dirt yard.

I Wonder . . .
I wonder what Corey was thinking and feeling when he found his father's old home . . .

Another Name, Another Clue

Corey knocked on the door. A thin woman appeared from inside the house. A small child, wearing only a diaper, stood beside her. "I don't want any," she said and closed the door in Corey's face.

Corey lifted his hand to knock again. "Please," he whispered. "Give me a chance."

She opened the door again, but she didn't look happy.

"I . . . I'm sorry to bother you," Corey said. "But I'm trying to find out about my father."

Her face softened for a second. Then the scowl returned. "What's with you? I can't even tell my own kids about their father."

"My father lived here—in this house," Corey said. "Maybe you've heard of him. Bill—William—Pony—Kemp."

The woman shifted in the doorway. "Humph, Billy Kemp. I haven't thought about him for years. Heard he died or somethin'."

Corey nodded. "He had cancer."

"I'm sorry," she said. "Billy was a good kid. One of the best. Always talking to the rest of us 'bout Jesus. Almost took him up on it."

Corey felt a wave of pride wash over him.

I Wonder . . .
I wonder what is different about people who love Jesus . . .

Those who do what is right are holy, just as Christ is holy.

1 John 3:7b

A Son of His Father

The woman opened the door wider. "Ya wanna come in? See the house?"

Corey followed her into the small house.

"Isn't much," she said. "Specially for me with four kids. Now with Billy, it was only him and his mom."

"My grandmother?"

"Guess it was." The woman looked sorry for Corey for a minute. "Heard she prayed, but never went to church far as I could tell. Died before Billy finished high school."

Corey closed his eyes.

"Tough stuff, huh, kid."

Corey opened his eyes. "There are things that make me sad. But I do have a father. My dad and mom helped with that."

"I don't get it," she said.

"It's God. He's my father too. I talk to him. It's sort of a gift—one that I'm just realizing my father wanted me to have."

"Humph," the woman said. "You're Billy's son, all right. Well, come back sometime. I wouldn't mind visiting again."

Corey shook hands with her. "I'll do that."

I Wonder . . .

I wonder what made the woman say, "You're Billy's son, all right" . . .

How great is the love the Father has given us so freely! Now we can be called children of God.

1 John 3:1a

Jesus Is Tempted

Luke 4:1-13

P ut yourself in this situation. When the teacher was giving the math lesson, you were finishing your social studies project that you forgot about last night. Now it is time to do your math paper, but you don't understand it. If you ask the teacher to explain it again, she'll be unhappy with you. If you go ahead and do it wrong, you'll get a bad grade. You feel trapped—until you think of an easy way out: you could just look at the paper of the person next to you.

Satan came to Jesus and told him easy ways to get bread to eat and prove that nothing could hurt him. But Jesus said no to all of Satan's ways.

What about you? Can you choose the right way instead of the easy ways of Satan? Do you know who wants to help you?

Song for the Week:
"What a Friend We Have in Jesus," *Songs for LiFE* 52

Prayer for the Week:
Jesus, you are perfect.
Thank you for saying no to wrong.
It is easier for me to do what is right
when I remember that you are there to help me.
Thank you for taking away my sins
because they come between God and me. Amen.

No More Free Afternoons

When Joshua Henry opened the front door, the October wind blew him inside with a whoosh of leaves. His mother shot him a disapproving look from the dinner table.

"Josh, this is the third evening in a row that you have been late for supper."

"From now on, you are to be home directly after school," his father said.

"It won't happen again," Josh said, squeezing into his chair without pulling it away from the table.

Caleb, Josh's younger brother, passed a plate of lasagna over to Josh. "I already did the praying."

Josh squinted his eyes at Caleb, stuck his tongue out, wiggled his head, and whispered, "You think you're so good."

While they ate, Mrs. Henry spoke. "Boys, I've taken on extra hours at work. Josh, I figured you're old enough to watch Caleb for an hour after school."

Josh mashed the cheesy top of his lasagna. "So you're punishing me?"

"You were late for supper again, so you have dish duty tonight," Mom said, "but staying home in the afternoons is simply what I need you to do for the family."

Josh wanted to scream "Not fair!" but he figured it'd get him nowhere. What he needed was a plan. No, he needed to bribe Caleb into staying home by himself and keeping quiet about it.

I Wonder . . .
I wonder if it's sometimes hard for you to obey too . . .

> He [Jesus] suffered when he was tempted. Now he is able to help others who are being tempted.
>
> *Hebrews 2:18*

Caleb-Sitting

Josh nearly walked on Caleb's heels all the way home from school the next day. He didn't let Caleb stop to pick up a red leaf off the sidewalk or let him follow a squirrel with puffed-out cheeks.

"Sometimes you're mean," Caleb said when they reached their front porch.

Josh unfolded a dollar bill that he had been holding in his hand. "Want it?"

"Sure!" Caleb held out his hand. Then he pulled back. "What's the catch?"

"No catch," Josh said. "Just take care of yourself while I do something."

"You're leaving me home alone, aren't you?"

Josh unlocked the front door, and they both went inside. "Listen," he said. "I have an after-school job for a couple of weeks. I'll split my money with you if you can pretend that I'm home with you."

"You mean lie?"

Josh waved the dollar bill in Caleb's face. "No, just earn this dollar by keeping quiet. It's simple."

Caleb took the dollar from Josh. He studied it. "A dollar a day?"

"You got it," Josh said. It was a big price to pay to keep his after-school job a secret. But he wanted money to spend the way he wanted to spend it—wild money.

I Wonder . . .
I wonder if there's a better way for Josh to keep his job . . .

> Nothing God created is hidden from him. His eyes see everything.
>
> *Hebrews 4:13a*

The Cover-Up

We have a high priest [Jesus] who can feel it when we are weak and hurting.

Hebrews 4:15a

Josh was on his way home when he saw his mom's car coming up Thistle Lane. His mind tried to tell his feet what to do. After a long, panicky minute, he spied Mr. Ingel's shrubs. He dived into the prickly underbrush. From his view between the branches, he watched his mom pull into the garage. When the car disappeared into the mouth of the garage, he ran across the street and into his backyard. He leaped over the deck railing and pulled on the sliding-glass door handle. Locked. He banged. Caleb remained sprawled out in front of the TV.

Josh picked up a handful of pebbles and tossed them against the glass.

This time he got Caleb's attention, and the door unlocked. Josh slipped into the family room just as Mom walked into the kitchen.

"Hello, boys," Mom said. "Everything go all right?"

"Super," Josh said. "Caleb was a good kid."

Mom stepped into the family room. "I'm proud. . . ." She grabbed onto a bag of chips and an empty soda can. "Josh, I left a note for you to fix apples and cheese for a snack."

Josh dug his fingernails into his palms. "I . . . I uh . . ."

Caleb said, "I can't read." Then he ran from the room.

I Wonder . . .
I wonder if it is easier to lie to get out of trouble or to tell the truth . . .

Getting Rid of a Lie

Josh tried out several stories in his mind. But they all had holes bigger than he could cover up.

He threw a sofa pillow on the floor. "I don't know why everything is my fault."

Mom stooped over to get the pillow. "Josh, I think you're overreacting. Next time just fix Caleb a healthy snack."

Josh left for his room and flung himself on the bed. Caleb knocked on the door.

"What do ya want?" Josh asked.

Caleb tossed the dollar bill at Josh. It floated to the floor. "I don't want this. It's not a good idea to fool Mom."

"I have responsibilities," Josh said. "Shadow and Pinecone will go hungry if I don't feed them."

"That's your job?" Caleb asked. "Feeding a dog and a cat. Wow!"

Josh felt his importance in Caleb's eyes. He shifted to a sitting position. "The Ingels went on a trip."

"If you tell Mom, I could help," Caleb said. "After school, I'd just go with you."

A section of stitching was loose on the quilt. Josh poked at it. Caleb might as well earn his money. Besides, having wild money was bringing him more trouble than fun. After they were paid, he and Caleb could go go-carting.

I Wonder . . .

I wonder if knowing you are not alone helps you tell the truth . . .

But build one another up every day. . . . Then you won't be fooled by sin's tricks.

Hebrews 3:13

Boldness

The next morning, Caleb overslept. There wasn't time for him to help Josh explain the pet-sitting job to Mom. Josh didn't mind. It'd give him a chance to prove to Mom he could do this job and watch Caleb too.

After school, Pinecone leaped off the sunny window ledge when Josh unlocked the Ingel's door. Shadow greeted the boys with a lick.

"I'll take Shadow for some exercise," Josh said. "You play with Pinecone."

Josh walked Shadow to the nature trail. A rabbit darted out from behind a rock. Shadow tugged against the leash. "Okay, boy. You can chase that bunny for a minute."

The short rabbit chase turned into fifteen minutes. When they finally got back to the Ingel's house, the door was wide open. Pinecone sat by his dish licking himself. But Caleb was gone. Josh searched the house and the yard. Still no Caleb. Then, with trembling fingers, Josh dialed the number for his mom's work. "I lost Caleb."

"I'll be home in a minute."

As he hung up the phone, Caleb walked into the Ingel's house carrying a ball of yarn from home. "I got this for Pinecone."

Just then, Mom's car sped into their driveway across the street. Caleb ran to tell her the whole story. Josh knew he was ready to talk too.

I Wonder . . .
I wonder how Josh will feel when he tells his mom the truth . . .

I wonder how his mom will feel . . .

So let us boldly approach the throne of grace. . . . We will find grace to help us.

Hebrews 4:16

Jesus Calls Peter

Luke 5:1-11

We all have many choices to make. Perhaps you want to be a gymnast, so you need to choose the right leotards. Or maybe you want to be a basketball player, so you need to choose a certain kind of shoe. You make a choice to follow and be like the heroes of your favorite activity. You want everyone to see the difference in you.

But what about choosing to be a Christian and follow Jesus? Does that make a difference in you—a difference people can see?

Peter knew in his heart that following Jesus makes all the difference in our lives. He told others about it when he confessed that Jesus is Lord.

Song for the Week:
"Take My Life," *Songs for LiFE* 74

Prayer for the Week:
Jesus, you are the way to God.
There is love and truth and heaven
when I follow you.
Take my heart and my mind
so that I can call you Lord. Amen.

A Difference?

Don't live any
longer the way
this world lives.

Romans 12:2a

Alexa Sanders put three barrettes in her hair—three on one side—a blue one, a red one, and a purple one. Being different was fun. Sometimes the other girls copied her, but that was fun too. She liked knowing that her ideas were popular.

After recess, Alexa noticed that Marisa Riley had three barrettes in her hair. Alexa didn't know much about Marisa. In fact, she didn't even notice Marisa until a few weeks ago when they prepared for the big Columbus Day program. Alexa had designed and painted cardboard ships for the show. And Marisa seemed to follow Alexa's every move.

Now, Alexa took out her colored pencil set. She sketched the dark brown leaves that hung onto the black branches of the scrub oak in Credo Canyon.

Marisa leaned forward from her seat behind Alexa. "Neat pencils."

"The best," Alexa said. "You can get a set at MacGiles for ten dollars."

Alexa smiled to herself. Probably Marisa would come with a set tomorrow. She'd show her how to use the sides and tips of the pencils for shading and outlining. But right now Marisa was slumping down in her seat. What was the matter?

Alexa turned around. Marisa needed a good laugh.

"Did you watch *Top Bunk* on TV last night?" Alexa asked. "It was so funny."

Marisa blinked. "You watch *Top Bunk*? I thought you were different. I mean, some people aren't allowed to watch it."

I Wonder . . .
I wonder why Marisa is surprised about what Alexa watches on TV . . .

An Example

Alexa unsnapped the barrettes in her hair. She played with them in her hand. "Do you watch *Top Bunk?*"

Marisa pressed down on her pencil eraser and rubbed until she made a hole in her paper. "Sure, I watch it. But my mom doesn't care what I do. We don't go to church or anything."

Church. The word stuck in Alexa's ears the rest of the afternoon.

At the end of the school day, Alexa found a wadded-up note in her cubby. She unfolded it.

> *I thought you were different because you went to church. You know, different like Betsy, Meghan, and Kalle.*

Alexa looked around the room to find Marisa. She was gone. And Alexa didn't even know where Marisa lived. She kicked against her backpack. The other girls weren't so perfect either. It wasn't right for Marisa to judge her just because of a TV show. So what if the characters were rude and used God's name carelessly? That didn't mean everyone who watched the show did the same.

She would just have to check for herself. Check to see what Betsy, Meghan, and Kalle watched on TV. And check to see if there was anything that made them different enough for Marisa to see.

I Wonder . . .
I wonder if it is possible to see a difference in people who follow Jesus . . .

Let your way of thinking be completely changed.

Romans 12:2b

The First Test

Test what God
wants for you.

Romans 12:2c

Alexa stopped at the Barna's house. Plenty of noises escaped from the inside of the house, but no TV noises. She pounded on the door. Then she felt a tapping on her elbow.

Quickly she turned around. "Drew Barna!"

Drew laughed. "Fooled you. I came behind you instead of answering the door."

Alexa put her hands on her hips. How could Betsy stand having two pesky younger brothers, plus Molly, and another foster sister coming soon?

"Did you want to see Betsy?" Drew asked.

"What do you think?" Alexa said.

"Well, she's mighty busy. Lucas has troubles with reading. Me and Betsy have to help him."

"Betsy and I," Alexa said, correcting him.

"That's the problem with I helping him," Drew said. "I'm in kindergarten and he's in first grade."

Alexa stomped her feet on the porch. "Well, let me in so I can see Betsy."

Drew ran around the side of the house. Soon he appeared at the front door and opened it wide for Alexa.

As Alexa listened to Lucas stumble over words, she decided that Betsy had more than enough patience for Lucas. Was that a difference that Marisa saw in Betsy?

I Wonder . . .
I wonder what makes Betsy so patient with her little brothers . . .

More Tests

Betsy turned her wheelchair to face Alexa. "Lucas tries until he gets it right."

Alexa forced a smile. "Do you know Marisa Riley from school?"

"I'm trying," Betsy said. "I've invited her over, but her mom hasn't given her permission yet."

"Why not?"

Betsy wheeled her chair closer to Alexa. "I don't know, but I think she needs a friend."

Alexa excused herself when Lucas wanted help with another word.

Across the street, Meghan was taking out the trash. She sang as she rolled the barrel to the curb. As Alexa waved at her, she remembered how she had grumbled the last time it was her turn to take out the trash. But Meghan probably sang because she was always singing. Not because she was happy taking out the trash. Or was this a difference that Marisa saw in Meghan?

"Meghan," called Alexa, running across the street. "Do you know Marisa Riley from school?"

Meghan gathered her brown curly hair into a ponytail. "Kinda. She told me she'd like to sing in the children's choir at church, but she didn't come to practice. The next day, she said her mom wouldn't let her come."

I Wonder . . .
I wonder if you've noticed something about Alexa's friends . . .

What he wants is right.

Romans 12:2d

Alexa's Difference

After Alexa left Meghan she went home instead of going to Kalle's. She already knew that Kalle fixed up old toys, skates, and bikes. Then she just gave them away. Who could beat that?

Alexa went into her garage. Half of their garage was for art activities. Her mom's kiln and pottery wheel. Alexa's easels, paints, and paper.

She clothespinned a new sheet of paper on the easel. She wanted to paint a picture that talked to her. Sometimes that happened—the painting took over and helped her understand things she couldn't make sense of. She needed that now.

She felt small—probably because she was disappointed in herself compared to Betsy and Meghan. So she painted a girl—a girl almost like herself with long, cinnamon brown hair. The head was painted small—at the top of the paper. Then at the bottom of the paper she painted thin legs and small feet. The head stretched a long way up the paper from the feet, so she placed a large heart in the center of the paper.

Yes, that is what she wanted too—a large heart.

As the painting dried, Alexa's own heart almost seemed bigger, filled with a friendly feeling for Marisa. Then she took the painting off the easel. She placed her new set of watercolors in the center and wrapped the painting around it. Tomorrow she would give it to Marisa.

I Wonder . . .
I wonder who filled Alexa with lovingkindness and goodness . . .

Jesus Calls Matthew

Luke 5:27-32

Do you ever play follow the leader? When you do, you can't be looking at what's on the other side of the fence or what's happening down the street. You have to keep your eyes on the person you are following.

Jesus called Matthew to follow, and Matthew obeyed. Matthew didn't think about collecting taxes anymore. He gave all his attention and time to Jesus.

Jesus calls you to follow him too. So how do you do it? One girl said she had been wondering and wondering if God was in her heart. Then one day she closed her eyes. "Come into my heart," she prayed. After that she didn't wonder again. Instead she worked on being kind to her friends and remembering to be joyful without complaining.

Song for the Week:
"Discipleship," *Songs for LiFE* 233

Prayer for the Week:
Jesus, you see me.
You see what I do and say.
Some of it isn't so good.
But I want to change.
Help me to be your follower. Amen.

Good Enough?

The last thing Alexa put in her school pack was the watercolor set. She didn't want her books to sit on top of this gift for Marisa. She couldn't wait to see Marisa unwrap the paints. Marisa would be her friend for life after this gift!

At school Alexa hid the paints under her sweater. At just the right time, she'd give them to Marisa.

The first bell rang. Marisa walked through the classroom door. She wasn't wearing a coat. How strange. It was a chilly November morning in Credo Canyon. Then Alexa noticed something even worse. Marisa's T-shirt was wrinkled and slightly stained. That T-shirt had to have come from the dirty clothes' basket.

"Marisa," said Mrs. Page. "Come to my desk. We need a conference."

Alexa pretended to examine the rocks at the science table so she could listen to their conversation.

"Did you bring in your homework from yesterday?" Mrs. Page asked.

Marisa let her long bangs fall over her eyes.

"Your grades are dropping," Mrs. Page said. "I can't excuse this."

The watercolor set pressed against Alexa's side. Marisa might not know how to take care of a new set.

I Wonder . . .
I wonder what Alexa is thinking about Marisa . . .

They [God's people] must consider the needs of others.

Titus 3:2b

Leads Against Marisa

Kalle Merton joined Alexa at the science table. "See how round this rock is?" Kalle said, holding a small, ball-shaped rock.

"What?" Alexa said. She was still thinking about Marisa.

"It might be a geode," Kalle said. "I found it up on Dragon Hill."

Alexa finally noticed what Kalle held in her hand. "What is it?"

"It could be a geode with crystals inside."

"Wow," Alexa said. "Break it open."

"I brought it for the whole class to see," Kalle said.

A group quickly formed around the science table.

"Most likely it's a sandstone that has collected bits and pieces over time," Mrs. Page said. "But let's crack it open."

Alexa noticed Marisa pushed herself close to the rock and Mrs. Page. Too bad she couldn't just tap Marisa on the head and see what kind of person she was inside.

A few hits with a hammer split the rock. Inside there were swirls of brown shades. Everyone groaned in disappointment and returned to their seats. But Alexa noticed Marisa put the pieces in her pocket.

Alexa nudged Kalle and told her what Marisa did.

Kalle whispered back to Alexa, "I don't trust her."

I Wonder ...

I wonder if you know someone like Marisa ...

I wonder if it would be hard for you to be a friend to Marisa ...

At one time we too acted like fools.

Titus 3:3a

Sneaky

Alexa laid the watercolor set in the bottom of her backpack. But her thoughts kept returning to her heart picture wrapped around the paint set. Did keeping the gift mean that her heart wasn't kind and generous after all? She had to find out more about Marisa.

After school she caught up with Kalle. "Do you know where Marisa lives?"

Kalle pointed to the apartments across from the school yard.

"Let's follow her," Alexa said. "Maybe we can pick up a clue or two."

"I don't know," Kalle said. "What if she sees us?"

Alexa played with the zipper on her backpack. "She took your pieces of the rock. Don't you want to know if you can trust her?"

"You're right," Kalle said.

Just past the flagpole they saw Marisa talking to a younger girl. Alexa knew the girl. It was a first grader, Jennifer Jordan. On Wednesdays Alexa listened to the first graders read. Alexa and Kalle moved closer to Marisa and Jennifer.

"I told you no," Marisa said. Her voice was close to a scream. Then she pushed Jennifer forward and they walked toward the apartments.

I Wonder . . .
I wonder if it is easy for you to know how God wants you to treat others . . .

Friends

Right after Marisa and Jennifer crossed the field and entered the apartment building, Alexa and Kalle did the same.

Once Alexa and Kalle were inside the building, they heard Marisa's voice in the stairwell. It sounded as if it came from the second floor. Alexa and Kalle ran up the steps. They turned down the hallway just in time to see a door close.

"I bet that's her apartment," Alexa said. She motioned for Kalle to come. Then Alexa put her head against the door.

Suddenly the door opened, and Marisa appeared.

Alexa stumbled forward, almost falling into the apartment.

"Alexa! Kalle!" Marisa said. "What—what are you doing here!?"

Alexa straightened up her body, but now her mind stumbled. What was she doing? Then she thought of the watercolors that were still in her backpack. She tugged on the zipper. "I—I have a present for you."

A voice called from inside. "Marisa, who is at the door?"

Marisa turned her head toward the apartment. "Friends—from school."

Friends. Marisa called them friends. Alexa's heart lightened. Maybe the watercolors were the right thing.

I Wonder . . .

I wonder who felt the happiest—Alexa or Marisa . . .

He saved us. It wasn't because of the good things we had done.

Titus 3:5a

Messes and Masterpieces

"Come in," Marisa said. She kicked a laundry basket out of the way. "I was on my way to the basement—to do some wash."

Alexa and Kalle stepped inside. A blonde woman wearing a short skirt placed a diaper-only baby into a playpen.

"My mom, Darcy Jordan," Marisa said, as if she needed to explain. "She picked up baby Renny from daycare. But she has to go back to work now."

Jordan, thought Alexa. That's Jennifer's last name. They must be stepsisters.

Jennifer came over and slipped her hand into Alexa's. "Listen to me read." She led Alexa to the sofa. They cleared off a pile of laundry.

"I'm sorry everything is such a mess," Marisa said, joining them on the sofa. "Renny has been fussy the last few days, so I don't get the work done."

Kalle took Renny out of the playpen. She played with the baby on the floor.

Alexa took the watercolors out of her backpack. She squeezed the plastic box through the layer of paper. Then she put it on Marisa's lap.

Marisa carefully unfolded the paper. When she saw the paints, she lifted the lid and slid her fingers over the smooth colors. "I can't believe it," she said. Then she reached under the sofa and lifted up a box. In the box were pictures drawn with plain pencil, but full of details.

I Wonder . . .
I wonder if sometimes you need Jesus to make your heart kinder . . .

> We were born again. The Holy Spirit gave us new life.
>
> *Titus 3:5c*

Jesus Calls Us

Luke 6:12-19, 27-36

Do you have a long list of people you love? That list might include parents, grandparents, aunts and uncles, cousins, neighbors, teachers, and friends. It might even include a dog or cat. So you know there is lots of love inside of you. But no matter how much love you already have, it can grow even more.

When Jesus calls you to follow him, he asks you to love. That may include loving a person who is hard to love. Or it may include loving a person who doesn't like you. Where do you get that kind of love?

Ask Jesus to give you love for someone who is difficult to love. Does it work?

Song for the Week:
"The Servant Song," *Songs for LiFE* 248

Prayer for the Week:
Jesus, all love comes from you.
You want us to be loving like you.
Show us this week how to add
   to our love.
Fill my heart with love
   for _____,
for your kingdom is full
   of love. Amen.

A Decision

Late in October, a letter arrived at the Barna house. The letter described an eight-year-old girl who needed a home. So the Barna family had a meeting to discuss what they should do.

Mrs. Barna passed around the picture of Ellie Coman. "The report says that Ellie needs a strong, loving home. She has caused problems in the past —stealing, lying, and running away."

Mr. Barna stroked his mustache. "Ever since Molly joined us as a baby, this family seemed completed," he said.

"But if no one else wants Ellie, where will she go?" Betsy asked.

"The social worker will find a place," Mrs. Barna said. "Besides, our bedrooms are full. Where would she sleep if she came here?"

"In the boys' room," Drew said. "Lucas and I could move into the tree house."

"Me too," Molly said.

Betsy tried to imagine what would have happened if the Barnas had not adopted her. When she was five years old, her foster family said that a girl with spina bifida was too much trouble. Betsy bowed her head. She wished that no one had to be called "too much trouble."

I Wonder . . .
I wonder what it feels like to have no one who loves and cares for you . . .

Serve the Lord.
When you hope,
be joyful.

Romans 12:11b-12a

Ellie

Once the decision was made to accept Ellie, Betsy and Mrs. Barna worked in Betsy's room. They rearranged the furniture, adding a second bed and a dresser.

The morning of Ellie's arrival, Betsy wheeled her chair between the beds. It was a tight fit. She lowered herself onto the floor beside her bed. She tugged at the under-the-bed box. There was just enough room to lift the lid of the box and pull out a turquoise bear. This was the bear that waited on her bed when she first came to the Barna's.

She placed the turquoise bear on Ellie's bed. Ellie could keep the bear as long as she needed it. She could talk to it at night—tell the bear how glad she was to have a home.

And soon people would say Ellie was no trouble. In fact, she brought joy to all.

Betsy climbed back into her chair just before a tap sounded on the bedroom door.

"Betsy," Mrs. Barna said. "Ellie is here."

The door opened and a thin girl dressed in white with gold chains around her neck walked in beside Mrs. Barna.

"Ellie, this is Betsy," Mrs. Barna said. "Betsy has set up her room just for you. Why don't you girls get acquainted?" Then Mrs. Barna left.

Ellie stood in the spot where Mrs. Barna left her. "So do you drool too? I hate stupid-looking people who can't even walk."

Betsy's welcoming smile trembled across her face.

I Wonder . . .

I wonder if Betsy will change her mind about Ellie . . .

When you suffer, be patient.

Romans 12:12b

The Prayer Journal

"You—you can put your things on this bed," Betsy said, pointing to the new bed in her room.

"Yeah, right. If you take off that stupid bear."

Betsy wheeled over to Ellie's bed and removed the turquoise bear.

Ellie bounced her suitcase on the bed. Then she sat beside her suitcase. "So, you have any fun in this joint? Of course you're stuck in that wheelchair, so it doesn't matter."

Betsy gripped the sides of her chair. Holding onto the wheel rims with all her strength kept her from saying hurting words back to Ellie. "You have more necklaces than I have ever seen at one time," Betsy finally said.

"Do you think they make me look like a movie star?"

"A movie star? Well, yeah. Sure."

"You wouldn't be lying to me, would you?" Ellie asked.

Betsy considered saying that movie star producers hired unusual characters, but she didn't think Ellie wanted to hear that. But before Betsy thought of what to say, Ellie was roaming the room and poking through Betsy's belongings.

"What's this?" she asked, holding up a cloth-covered book.

"My prayer journal," Betsy whispered. "I've been praying for you too. Ever since I knew about you."

I Wonder . . .

I wonder if Betsy's prayers for Ellie will change . . . or will they stop . . .

When you pray, be faithful.

Romans 12:12c

Ellie's Necklaces

Mrs. Barna entered the bedroom. "Ellie, is Betsy helping you get settled?"

Ellie dropped the prayer journal on the desk. "Oh, Mrs. Barna, I'd much sooner help your Betsy than have her help me. It just isn't fair that she is the way she is, but now that I'm here, she'll have all the help she needs."

Mrs. Barna opened her mouth, but no words came out. She turned to Betsy with a puzzled look across her face.

"It's okay, Mom," Betsy said. "Do you need help with supper?"

"Oh, let me help," Ellie said.

"I ordered pizzas," Mrs. Barna said. "I'll call you when they come."

As Mrs. Barna turned around to leave, Ellie rolled her eyes.

"What a mother. I'm glad my mother isn't like her."

"Do you know your mother?" Betsy asked.

"Of course. Who do you think gave me all these necklaces? When she finds my dad, we are all going to live together."

Betsy wondered what kind of mother sent flashy necklaces. Then Betsy remembered that the information about Ellie reported no contact with her mother.

"Come on," Betsy said. "Let's ask if we can eat in the family room. Dad'll build a fire in the fireplace, too, if we ask."

I Wonder . . .
I wonder if it's hard for Betsy to be kind to Ellie . . .

Welcome others into your homes.

Romans 12:13b

Thanks for Ellie

Be joyful with those who are joyful. Be sad with those who are sad.

Romans 12:15

Mr. Barna stacked the wood in the fireplace. The flame from the match quickly burst into a big flame on the crumpled newspaper.

The flames flickered in Betsy and Ellie's eyes as they watched the logs catch on fire. Betsy's thoughts strayed to dreams. She knew what dreams about a mother were like. The details of her dream changed over time, but basically it was the same. The mother who gave up Betsy at birth one day woke up and realized she had missed out. This mother gave up job, money, and home just to find her daughter. And every year that passed just proved the search was long and difficult. But when the mother found Betsy, she said the search was worth it all.

"Pizzas," called Mrs. Barna.

Lucas, Drew, and Molly sat around the coffee table. Mrs. Barna set the steaming pizza boxes in the middle of the table.

Ellie lifted a lid. She reached for a wide slice.

Mrs. Barna gently placed her hand over Ellie's hand. "We pray before we eat."

"My mother taught me how to pray," Ellie said. She closed her eyes.

The Barnas looked at each other while Ellie sat there with her eyes closed.

Then Betsy said, "I'll pray. Dear Jesus, thank you for this food. And thank you for bringing Ellie to us. Amen."

I Wonder . . .
I wonder how Ellie can tell that the Barna family belongs to Jesus . . .

Jesus Heals a Man Who Can't Walk

Luke 5:17-26

Y ou trust your best friend to keep a secret. You trust that your mom will listen to you. Without people to trust, you would be miserable.

The man who couldn't walk in this week's story gave up all his misery when he trusted Jesus. He gave up his useless legs. He gave up his sinful heart. He gave it all to Jesus. And Jesus gave him working legs and a joyful heart.

Jesus wants you to know that you can trust him too. He knows that if you believe in him, you will have as much joy as the man who was healed.

Song for the Week:
"If You Believe and I Believe,"
Songs for LiFE 242

Prayer for the Week:
Savior and Lord,
you have set us free.
More than anything you want
us to know that you are God
and that you want to save us.
Send your peace and
healing to _____,
for you are Savior and
Lord. Amen.

The Challenge

After the pizzas were gone, the Barna family played Monopoly. Drew and Lucas lost their money early in the game. Ellie was out next. When she laughed with the boys about losing, Betsy's hopes rose. Maybe Ellie could fit into the family after all.

"It's time for bed," said Mr. Barna, checking his watch. "In the morning we'll have a big breakfast. Then off to church and Sunday school. How does that sound, Ellie?"

"I'm hungry already. And I love church and Sunday school." She threw them kisses as if she were a movie star leaving the stage. Then she disappeared to the bedroom.

Betsy followed slowly in her chair. Supper and games were fun, but a small fear did a forward roll in her stomach. Which Ellie would she find in her room?

Her chair pushed the door open. Ellie sat up straight at the foot end of the bed.

"I'm telling you now," Ellie said. "I'm not going to any old church. So you better think of an excuse for me. Tell them I'm sick or whatever."

"I won't lie for you," Betsy said.

"Com'mon. Think of something good. Then we'll both get out of it."

"My friends go to church," Betsy said. "We sing. And we pray for each other."

"Prayer. Yeah, right. If that worked, you'd pray to walk." Ellie scraped a red fleck off her painted nails. "But I'll tell you what. If you pray for a miracle in front of your friends, I'll go with you just to see what happens."

I Wonder . . .
I wonder if Betsy has ever prayed to God for a miracle . . .

Help me always to tell the truth about how faithful you are.

Psalm 119:43a

The Dream and the Lame Man

Betsy had mastered her bedtime routine, but tonight she moved awkwardly. At last she rolled into bed. Ellie busied herself with placing her necklaces over the dresser-drawer knobs.

Usually Betsy knelt beside her bed for prayers. Tonight she saved them until she buried her head in the pillow.

"Jesus, what am I going to do tomorrow?" Betsy breathed her prayer into the pillow. "Do you want me to walk? I've never been this sad. Be with me."

Even through the darkness of the pillow, Betsy knew when Ellie put off the light. Ellie didn't bother Betsy as she climbed into the other bed. Betsy relaxed her stiffened body. Then she drifted back into her prayer.

A strangely dressed man appeared in her mind as she tried to pray. "It happened to me," he said.

"Who are you?" Betsy asked.

"The lame man. The one Jesus healed. But first he forgave my sins. Everything wrong was completely wiped out. From that day on, I lived with joy."

Now was her chance to ask the big question.

"What about the walking?" Betsy asked.

"That was great too. But my clean heart is what really changed my life."

I Wonder . . .
I wonder what God wants for us most of all . . .

> My sadness has worn me out. Give me strength as you have promised.
>
> *Psalm 119:28*

Betsy's Peace

At 6 A.M., Betsy slipped out of bed. The muscles in her neck and arms were stiff. She had told Jesus last night that joy in her soul was more important than walking. But why did her body have to remind her of pain this morning?

Ellie was still sleeping. Betsy pivoted around on the floor. It was quieter than using her chair. She selected her dark green pantsuit to wear. The embroidered red rose on the collar always made her feel special. She added her cross necklace.

"I see you dressed for church," Ellie said with a yawn. "Does that mean you're going for the prayer?"

Betsy climbed into her chair. "I don't need to walk. In fact, sometimes my handicap helps me. It—it makes me think about what is really important."

"You're a fake," Ellie said. "Everyone wants to walk."

"Girls, are you ready?" called Mrs. Barna.

Ellie scrambled into a white sweatsuit that had appliqued gold stars on the front.

After a breakfast of Mr. Barna's waffles with berries, Drew and Lucas took charge of Ellie. They ushered her to the van.

On her way past Betsy, Ellie whispered, "Guess what. I'm going, but I don't have to stay 'cause you're scared to pray."

I Wonder . . .
I wonder what Ellie needs to learn about praying . . .

Sunday School

"Mrs. Barna," Ellie said as they drove to church, "even though I'm in third grade and Betsy's in fourth, may I be in her class?"

"That's a great idea," Mrs. Barna said. "I'm so glad you two are friends already."

Betsy closed her eyes. "Lord, you've been so good to me. You have given me friends and a family. But now it seems as if this girl is taking over my family. Do you still love me?"

When they got to church, Drew and Lucas almost forgot to help Betsy with her wheelchair. They were so excited about telling Ellie all their stories. But two minutes before 9 o'clock, Ellie silently followed Betsy to the fourth-grade classroom. Within seconds, everyone gathered around Ellie.

"She is a sweet kid," Alexa said. "I'd even like her for my sister."

Mrs. Ingel, their teacher, came into the room. Everyone found a chair in the circle.

After Mrs. Ingel prayed, Alexa jumped up. "Hey, Ellie's missing."

"She wasn't planning on staying," Betsy said.

"What's the matter, Sugar?" Mrs. Ingel asked Betsy. "You seem so sad."

"It's Ellie. She says I should want to walk. And she wants me to pray for it. Today."

I Wonder . . .

I wonder if you feel sad for Betsy . . .

I wonder what you would say to her if you were her friend . . .

Lord you are everything I need. . . . Be kind to me as you have promised.

Psalm 119:57-58

Betsy's Legs

Mrs. Ingel placed her hand over Betsy's hand. "Last night I woke up thinking about you. I didn't know why, but now I know it was God's plan. Anyway, I came up with an idea—a fun way for you to move. Legs for you to borrow."

At that moment, Ellie jumped out of the closet. "This can't be happening." Trevor, Peter, Kalle, Alexa, and Meghan all started talking at once.

"Well, it's no use staying in the classroom," Mrs. Ingel said. "Follow me." So the class put on their coats and followed Mrs. Ingel to the stables.

"The horses," Mrs. Ingel said. "Betsy can ride a horse."

The stable owner, Mr. Clover, welcomed them. When Mrs. Ingel explained what she wanted, he helped Betsy on top of Specks, his prize horse. Warm steam rose from Specks's nostrils in the chilly stable. Mr. Clover found horses for the others too.

"Look at me," Betsy said. "I'm on legs. And the same height as everyone else."

"Come back when you have time to ride," Mr. Clover said. "The movement of the horse will be good for you. It'll help you walk smoother when you use leg braces too."

"Ellie, can you believe this?" Betsy asked.

Ellie warmed her hands against the horse's sides. "Don't think this changes anything. Maybe God heard you, maybe not. But God will never listen to me."

I Wonder . . .
I wonder if God listens to all prayers . . .

God, you will gladly accept a heart that is broken because of sadness over sin.

Psalm 51:17b

Jesus Heals the Centurion's Servant

Luke 7:1-10

It's not fun to be sick. Sometimes it's even scary.

When Jesus walked on the earth, being sick was even scarier. Many of the doctors in that day were more like magicians than physicians. They might have given you seven hairs from seven old dogs to make you well.

So it's no wonder that crowds of sick people followed Jesus. Finally there was someone who could make a sick person well. And it wasn't magic.

Jesus cares about us and our bodies too. He knows when we need help because our body is ill. He is the great healer.

Song for the Week:
"Be Still and Know," *Songs for LiFE* 225

Prayer for the Week:
Jesus, you are the great doctor.
When I am sick, make me well.
Take care of _____ who is sick.
Keep our bodies strong so we can serve you.
Keep our hearts clean so we can live with
   you. Amen.

Ellie's Troubles

Are any of you in trouble? Then you should pray.

James 5:13a

Ellie ran from the stables and back to Credo Canyon Church. By now she should have been able to make Betsy cry and be miserable. Stupid Betsy in her wheelchair didn't have the right to be happy. But no matter what happened, Betsy prayed and everything worked out. Well, it didn't work out for Ellie.

But right now she had to get out of going to church. Life was unhappy enough without sitting in church. She found Mrs. Barna.

"I can't stay for church," Ellie said. "I'm feeling sick."

Mrs. Barna touched her forehead. "You do feel a bit warm. I'll drive you home."

It would have been a silent ride home, except that Ellie groaned every few minutes.

"Go ahead and get in bed," Mrs. Barna said. "I'll get the thermometer."

Ellie gargled hot water from the bathroom sink. Then she climbed into bed.

Mrs. Barna came in and sat on the edge of the bed. She placed the thermometer under Ellie's tongue. While the thermometer stuck out of Ellie's mouth, Mrs. Barna rubbed Ellie's hand.

Mrs. Barna took the thermometer out. "Hmmm," she said. "You don't have a fever." She touched her lips to Ellie's forehead. "Rest for now. I'll check on you again." Then she left.

Ellie closed her eyes. How long before she'd be found out as a liar and a fake?

I Wonder . . .

I wonder why Mrs. Barna was so gentle with Ellie . . .

Sick!

Ellie slept for an hour. When she woke up, she heard voices in the house. Everyone must be home from church.

She pushed off the covers and jumped out of bed. Whoa. She gripped the bedpost. It was as if she had jumped off a merry-go-round. Then her topsy-turvy stomach tightened. She ran to the bathroom.

In a minute, Mrs. Barna was by her side. "It's okay, Ellie. I'm here to take care of you."

When Ellie's stomach was empty, Mrs. Barna held Ellie on her lap. Then she washed Ellie with a warm, wet cloth. Ellie dropped her head against Mrs. Barna. It was hard for Ellie to stop shaking, but Mrs. Barna held her close.

With the warm arms wrapped around her, Ellie wondered if she got sick because she lied about being sick. Betsy would know. Betsy knew about God. Mrs. Barna carried her to the bed and tucked the blankets around her. Ellie sank her head into the pillow.

Then she heard the squeak of Betsy's chair.

"Dear Jesus," Betsy said. "Please make Ellie better, soon. And let her know that she isn't too much trouble. And that she can be forgiven for lying or anything else."

I Wonder . . .
I wonder how Betsy's prayer made Ellie feel . . .

The prayer offered by those who have faith will make you well.

James 5:15a

Trust

"Not too much trouble." Ellie repeated those words "not too much trouble" over and over in her mind. But "too much trouble" is what all the other foster homes said about her. Why didn't Betsy think that too? Ellie had tried her hardest to make trouble for Betsy. If she felt better, she'd try right now, and try harder. After all, this was Betsy's room, and if she didn't make trouble for Betsy, then Betsy for sure would make it hard for her. That's the way it worked, didn't it? Maybe Betsy was different. But Ellie couldn't take that chance.

Betsy is a . . . There had to be something bad she could say to Betsy. But her head hurt. And she was so cold. She curled up under the blankets. Maybe she was getting sicker.

Betsy's chair moved. "Please don't leave me alone," she wanted to say to Betsy, but she couldn't manage to say anything.

But Betsy didn't leave. Instead, she placed another blanket over Ellie. Almost immediately the blanket trapped the heat, and Ellie stopped shivering. Then a hand took her hand. She squeezed the fingers that held hers. Now she didn't feel afraid.

Betsy had prayed for her. And God listened to Betsy. Ellie just wanted to sleep and start over with tomorrow.

I Wonder . . .
I wonder how God will answer Betsy's prayer for Ellie . . .

The Lord will heal you.

James 5:15b

Prayer Power

When Ellie woke up, the bedroom was bright and sunny. The alarm clock on the table between the two beds read 10:41. Ellie sat up all the way. Next to the clock was a note with her name on it.

Dear Ellie: I hope you feel better today. Lucas and Drew went to school with me. Molly is home with Mom. She promised to check on you every hour. Mom will tell her when. Love, Betsy.

Ellie read the note over. Betsy signed the note with love. If only she could be sure of that love. Some people were good at covering up their true feelings. Betsy could be one of those people. Then Ellie spied Betsy's journal on the window seat. It was tucked underneath the turquoise bear.

10:47. She had thirteen minutes before Molly came. Two pages from the back, Ellie saw her name. She read the entry.

At our family meeting, we talked about making room for Ellie Coman. I think Mom and Dad would have said no if I didn't want to share my room. Mom and Dad have given me so much. The operations, the wheelchair, my room—the only room in the house with its own bathroom and without steps to climb. Any other mom or dad would have made my room their room. Sometimes it makes me cry, but I can't cry—I have to share. That's the best way to show how thankful I am. What if I didn't have a home where I was loved? My first mom thought I was ugly and disgusting. She wouldn't even keep me for a week. Dad Barna says I'm beautiful. He wanted me to have my last operation so I could sit tall and pretty. What if there is no one to love Ellie? Mom says some days it will be very hard to love her. I can pray for help in loving her. I just know I can.

Ellie closed the journal.

I Wonder . . .

I wonder if God loves us—even when we're not very lovable . . .

> The prayer of a godly person is powerful. It makes things happen.
>
> *James 5:16c*

With Love

So admit to one another that you have sinned.

James 5:16a

Then, like a feather, Molly came to the door. "Peek-a-boo. I see you awake," Molly said. "I like you awake."

"Me too," Ellie said. "And I'm hungry, so I don't think I'm sick anymore."

"Yippee!" Molly said. "I'll go tell Mom."

Ellie reached for Molly's hand. "No, wait. Come sit by me first. I want to talk."

With a big grin, Molly climbed up on the window seat beside Ellie.

"Tell me about Betsy," Ellie said. "What do you like best about her?"

"The way she moves," Molly said.

Ellie rearranged the pillows that were behind her back. Little kids like Molly didn't understand much. The way Betsy moved was the worst part about her.

Molly hugged her knees up to her chest. "Betsy moves to be with you."

It's true, thought Ellie. Betsy rolled her chair beside others. It was as if she moved because she cared about you. It showed that she wanted to be with you. Ellie hugged Molly, and they went to get lunch.

After lunch, Ellie rested and waited for Betsy to come home from school.

When Betsy saw Ellie, she said. "You must be better."

"Yes," Ellie said. "Better all the way through. Thank you for praying for me. I—I want to be your friend. Please forgive me for being mean."

I Wonder . . .
I wonder if anyone has ever prayed for you . . . or if you pray for others . . .

Jesus Heals a Sick Woman

Luke 8:43-48

Can God be great and powerful and notice the little things at the same time? The woman who reached out to touch Jesus knew of God's great power, but she didn't know God cared about her. Jesus made sure she knew.

How about you? Do you believe that Jesus can care about you as well as all the students in your classroom and on your playground? Can he find you in a row of cars, busses, and trucks on the highway? Does he see you in a line of people waiting to be next?

Song for the Week:
"He's Got the Whole World,"
   Songs for LiFE 198

Prayer for the Week:
Father of Jesus and healer of our life,
your hand is larger than our world.
Your touch is closer than our mother.
Your eye notices each and every one.
Thank you for being great
and yet always staying close to us.
   Amen.

Plenty and More

There was one thing Ellie was sure about—God listened to Betsy. And somehow she needed to get God's attention too. Since Betsy had a prayer list, Ellie decided she also needed one. "I have fifteen things on my prayer list," she said. "Do you think I'll get them all?"

Betsy licked the envelope of a Christmas card. "What's on your list?"

"New shoes, an 'A' in math, pierced ears . . ."

"Prayer lists aren't like Christmas lists," Betsy said.

Ellie chewed the pink eraser on her pencil.

"Put Molly on your list," Betsy said. "On Saturday we're visiting her mom. It's a long drive into the city. But the hardest part is that Molly's mom doesn't always remember her daughter. She is so sick that her mind doesn't always work."

In the dark parts of Ellie's mind she wondered if her mother was sick too. Maybe that's why she never heard from her mother. She rearranged the chains around her neck. "Is Molly's mother in a hospital?"

"No," Betsy said. "A hospice. It's a house full of very sick people."

Maybe that was the problem. There were too many sick people. God needed people to keep track of everything for him on prayer lists.

I Wonder . . .
I wonder how God can notice and hear everyone who needs him . . .

Don't worry about anything. Instead, tell God about everything.

Philippians 4:6a

A Full House

On Saturday, Ellie dressed to go with Molly, Betsy, and Mrs. Barna to see Molly's mother. Betsy brought a deck of cards and played "Go Fish" with Molly in the car. Ellie brought her notebook.

As the Barna van left Credo Canyon and drove through the country and into the city, Ellie watched out the window. She knew she was born in the city. Her mother probably still lived there. Part of Ellie wished she'd find her mother in the hospice, but finding her in the restaurant when they stopped for lunch would be better. Ellie didn't know what her mother looked like, but "young and beautiful" stuck in her mind.

"Here we are," said Mrs. Barna as they stopped in front of a one-story ranch house in an ordinary neighborhood.

Ellie noticed the driveway led to a picture window instead of a garage door. This was her favorite kind of house. It used to be her dream that a family would change their garage into a room just for her. You're more important than a car, they'd say.

The notebook felt heavy in her hands. If she wrote down all her troubles and dreams, God would be busier than ever.

She followed Mrs. Barna, Betsy, and Molly to the front door. Molly was quieter than usual—almost sad. Would Molly's mother hug and love her daughter?

I Wonder . . .

I wonder if Ellie knows that God knows what she needs before she writes it in her notebook . . .

Ask and pray. Give thanks to him [God].

Philippians 4:6b

The Sick

Mrs. Barna rang the doorbell of the hospice house. A smiling lady wearing a pink sweater answered the door.

Ellie peeked around Mrs. Barna, Betsy, and Molly before entering. A Christmas tree stood in the middle of the first room. Once they were inside, Ellie saw a white-haired man and a very, small shriveled man sitting on a sofa. A woman who had plastic tubes connected from her nose to a tank sat on a side chair.

"Who are they?" Ellie whispered to Betsy.

Betsy took Ellie's hand. "This is Eddie, Jake, and Rose."

Ellie sat down between Eddie and Jake. "May I write down your names in my notebook?" Ellie asked. "I'm making a prayer list."

"Put down my daughter's name too." Rose said. "Pray that she'll come and visit me. I'm afraid she has forgotten she has a mother."

"No one forgets they have a mother," Ellie said. "I bet she doesn't know where you are."

"Then put her down for sure," Rose said. "Her name is Sharon."

"I will," Ellie said. But she wished she could tell Rose that mothers and daughters would always find each other because they belonged together.

I Wonder . . .
I wonder if Ellie feels as if she belongs to someone . . .

Then God's peace will watch over your hearts and your minds because you belong to Christ Jesus.

Philippians 4:7a

A Longer List

After Ellie wrote Rose, Sharon, Eddie, and Jake on her prayer list, she realized that Betsy, Molly, and Mrs. Barna had left the living room. She stood in the middle of the room. "They went down the hall," Jake said.

The hallway was decorated with quilts and pictures. There were four doorways. Ellie stepped into the first room. Tufts of white hair fell over a pink face. She tiptoed closer to the face. The eyes in the face stared at the ceiling.

"Hi, I'm Ellie. If you tell me your name, I'll put you on my prayer list."

The eyes shifted down and toward Ellie. "It's Sam. Someone came to pray for me on Tuesday. But it's nice to have a prayer on Saturday too."

She wrote "Sam" in her book.

The door across the hall was only half open. She pushed it open all the way and went inside. Molly and Betsy sat on the side of a bed with their feet dangling over the edge. A thin woman with long, black hair and copper skin sat across from them in a brown-plaid reclining chair.

"Soon it's my birthday," Molly said to the woman. "On Christmas day."

"I forgot," the woman said. "Is it really almost Christmas?"

Molly wiggled on the bed. "You wishes you had presents for me?"

The woman whom Ellie guessed was Molly's mom turned her face to the window.

I Wonder . . .

I wonder if God knows you even when no one else does . . .

My God will meet all your needs.

Philippians 4:19a

Belonging

Ellie turned around in the doorway. Her lost mother wouldn't have a present for her daughter either. She went down the hall and into the next room just for a place to go. A lady with bumpy gray hair sat in bed knitting and humming. Slowly Ellie walked up to the bed. "I'm Ellie. May I put your name on my prayer list?"

"Come here," said the woman. "I'd love to meet another Ellie who knows Jesus."

"I really don't know Jesus," Ellie said. "But I have a prayer list."

The woman put down her knitting. "If your name is Ellie, you must be here for a special reason, 'cause my name is Ellie too. You can call me Grandma Ellie."

Ellie had lived in six homes in her eight years, but this was the first time someone said, "Call me Grandma."

Grandma Ellie took Ellie's hand. "When I go to heaven, Jesus will want an Ellie from down here to talk to him. An Ellie-girl that belongs to him. You know that's what praying is all about—belonging to Jesus, talking to him, and giving him all your worries."

"Belong to Jesus." Ellie let that idea settle in her mind. If she belonged to Jesus, then Jesus would listen to her. Listen to everything she worried about today. Listen to all the troubles of the people she met—no matter how long the list became. That's what a prayer list was for—giving it to Jesus. Grandma Ellie knew exactly what an Ellie-girl needed.

I Wonder . . .
I wonder if you can trust that God wants to listen to you and the troubles on your list . . .

He will meet [your needs] in keeping with his wonderful riches that come to you because you belong to Christ Jesus.

Philippians 4:19b

Jesus Calms the Storm

Mark 4:35-41

Your heart beats faster when there is danger. You know that some things are just bigger than you. You can't control them. Even to trust Jesus isn't easy because you just don't know how things will turn out.

The disciples, caught in a dangerous storm on the sea, believed they might die. They wanted Jesus to wake up and worry with them. After all, they couldn't be calm in this storm. Or could they?

Song for the Week:
"When I Am Afraid," *Songs for LiFE* 218

Prayer for the Week:
When I am afraid,
the scary feelings get bigger and bigger.
But Jesus, you are greater
than anything that can scare me.
Instead of being afraid,
I'll talk to you.
I'll trust you.
I'll thank you for being with me. Amen.

The Storm

Peter Wit stood on the kitchen floor mat and stomped the snow off his sneakers.

The house was quiet, too quiet. Fast-falling, fat snowflakes muffled outside noises, but what made it so quiet inside?

"Mom. Zach. Nicky." No answers.

A red number 1 glowed on the answering machine. Peter pushed the play button.

"Time 2:05. Boys, this is Mom. I went to help Grandma Wit clean her house. We were so busy all morning that I didn't notice the storm. The forecast only predicted a couple of inches, but there are already six inches on the ground. Monument Hill has been closed, so I can't get home tonight. I called Dad. He's leaving work early, but the snow may slow him down. Be calm and be good. I'll call. . . . " The machine cut off the message with a screeching beep.

Peter's mind rushed through the afternoon. When school was dismissed early because of the storm, Zach and Nicky had been waiting for him outside his fourth-grade classroom. But Peter wanted to throw snowballs with the other boys in his class, so he sent Zach and Nicky home to tell Mom. Why weren't they here?

Peter switched on the TV for some noise. "Traffic is crawling along the Interstate," said a reporter, standing in swirling snow. That meant Dad wasn't coming home soon.

I Wonder . . .

I wonder if you can imagine how Peter feels . . .

My brothers and sisters, you will face all kinds of trouble.

James 1:2a

Hiding or Missing?

Peter picked up the phone to call Mom at Grandma's house. Next to the phone, Zach's backpack was stuffed into the corner beside the refrigerator. Those stinkers must be hiding from him. He put the phone down. "Zach. Nicky," he called. He held his breath for a second. Nothing.

He ran through the house. Not behind the sofa. Not in their room. Not in the basement. He opened the door to his parents' room and sprawled on the floor to lift up the bed skirt. Mom's Bible was under the bed, but no brothers. Mom always slipped her Bible under her bed after she prayed in the morning. Did she pray for her boys this morning? Peter believed she did. But it was hard to prove that right now. No one in the family seemed safe.

The hall closet. He should have thought of that before. But their mittens, hats, boots, and jackets were not there. Then Peter thought about the answering machine. It always beeped when there was a message. After someone listened to the message, the number of messages appeared in the little window, but there was no beep.

Had Zach and Nicky listened to the message and then left to look for him?

He arched his foot into his laced-up boots. He zippered his jacket as he stepped out into ribbons of dropping snow.

His footprints from earlier were gone. Everywhere it was white.

Your faith will be put to the test.

James 1:3a

I Wonder . . .

I wonder what difference it makes that Mrs. Wit prayed daily for her family . . .

Out in the Storm

Peter closed his eyes, pretending there was no storm, pretending he was walking to the Barna's house just like on any other day. When he thought he should be there, he opened his eyes. The world was as white and blinding as ever. He couldn't tell if he was there or not. Now he wished he had thought of calling Lucas and Drew to find out if they had seen Zach and Nicky.

"Help, help," he cried out against the wind. The wind picked up speed for a second and then it stopped. Not far ahead a fuzzy light glowed. He moved toward the light. His foot hit a hard surface—a porch step. He scrambled up the steps and pounded on the Barna's front door.

Warm air, light, popcorn smells, and Mrs. Barna greeted him.

"Who is this snowman?" asked Mrs. Barna.

"It's me. Peter from next door. Are Zach and Nicky here?"

"No. I haven't seen them all day. But come in," Mrs. Barna said. "Tell me what's wrong."

The melting snow that dripped off of Peter's body rolled down like tears as he told the story to Mrs. Barna.

"We need help," Mrs. Barna said. "Let me call Leo Ingel. Shadow is getting old, but he's still a mighty smart dog. Can pick up any scent."

I Wonder . . .
I wonder if Peter knows that God can see through snowstorms . . .

You know that when that happens it will produce in you the strength to continue.

James 1:3b

Prayers

Mrs. Barna called the family to pray while waiting for Mr. Ingel and Shadow.

"Dear Jesus, please scoop up Zach and Nicky out of the snow," prayed Drew.

"They're our friends, Jesus. We need to see them soon. 'Cause it hurts with them missing," prayed Lucas.

Peter could almost hear Nicky jabbering nonstop and Zach crashing around with his every move. Their sounds had bugged him yesterday. And the day before. He had wished that he didn't have two little brothers. But now he'd welcome those sounds.

When he heard Shadow barking outside, Peter opened the Barna's door against the white. He buttoned the flap over the jacket's zipper.

"Let's go to your house, Peter," said Mr. Ingel. "We need a sock or a shoe from Zach and Nicky for Shadow to smell."

Holding on to Shadow's leash with Mr. Ingel made the blinding walk easier. When they came to his house, Peter rushed to Zach and Nicky's room. He grabbed Zach's baseball cap. Zach wore it fishing and hiking. Shadow might even know it was Zach's cap. And Nicky's collector vest. It was really a fishing vest, but Nicky used the pockets to collect rocks, pinecones, and whatever caught his fancy.

Shadow barked and paced after sniffing the vest and cap. Then he ran to the door.

"We're going to find them, right boy?" Peter said.

I Wonder . . .

I wonder what kinds of things help you keep going when you feel discouraged . . .

> The strength to keep going must be allowed to finish its work.
>
> *James 1:4a*

Brothers for Keeps

Shadow stretched out in front of the door, blocking Peter and Mr. Ingel. "Come on, Shadow," Peter said. "We have to find Zach and Nicky."

Shadow growled and refused to move.

"The storm," Peter said. "Is Shadow afraid?"

Mr. Ingel ruffled Shadow around the neck. "Shadow's arthritis keeps him from chasing every rabbit, but he can still do it. I think he knows it's important to search for Zach and Nicky in the snow, but for some reason he doesn't want to."

Peter knelt beside Shadow. "Please boy, this is important. My brothers are the best friends I have. I don't always show that, but it's true."

Shadow put his head between his paws and whined.

"It's no use," Peter said. "I'll go by myself."

"That's foolish," Mr. Ingel said. "You'll get yourself lost."

Peter ran to the back door, but as he opened it Zach, Nicky, and Mr. Wit tumbled inside.

"Whoa, are we glad we found you," Zach said.

"Found me?" Peter asked. "You're the ones who are lost."

"No way," Nicky said. "When Dad came home, we left to go searching for you."

Peter leaned into his father's hug. Somehow they had all missed each other in the snow.

I Wonder . . .
I wonder if we sometimes forget that God is watching over us . . .

You will have everything you need.

James 1:4c

Jesus Heals a Little Girl

Mark 5:21-24, 35-43

When do you come to the end? The end of the school day means time to play, go to music lessons, gymnastics, or some other activity. So the end can mean the beginning of another thing.

The end of something you enjoy can be sad. That's why the end to life on earth can be sad. Jesus knew that too. But he showed that he was stronger than death when he brought the girl back to life. He again showed he was stronger than death when he came back to life himself. His power over death comes with a promise for you. After life on earth, he promises you life forever with him in heaven.

Be sad at the end of life on earth. But also be joyful in knowing it's the beginning of heaven.

Song for the Week:
"What Wondrous Love Is This"
Songs for LiFE 169

Prayer for the Week:
Jesus, make me ready for heaven.
Make me ready by knowing you now.
Put a song in my heart.
Put a picture of good things in my mind.
Take away the sadness that comes
from hurts and sicknesses.
And let me know that these little bits
of happiness will be forever in heaven.
Amen.

The News

"The end," Molly said as she closed the picture book. She had only looked at a few pages. It was one of those days when she wished Drew would hurry home from morning kindergarten.

Mom Barna had loads of laundry and baking to do this morning. She had told Molly to read the book by herself. Usually Mom Barna sat down with Molly to read while the older kids were in school.

Molly tiptoed to the kitchen. Just once more she'd ask if it was time for Drew to come home. She stopped when she heard her name. Mom was on the phone. Her voice sounded quiet and sad.

"Yes," Mom said. "I've been dreading this news. Molly understands that her mother was going to die, but still. . . ."

"Mom Tessa," whispered Molly. The mother who shared her brown eyes and dark skin but who was very sick. So sick she sent Molly to live with a family who could take care of a little girl as she grew up. So sick that Molly was told that soon there would be no more trips to the city. No more chances to hold Tessa's hand and touch her beautiful face.

Molly turned around. The door to the basement was open. She sat on the step and then went down one step at a time on her bottom.

I Wonder . . .
I wonder if you have ever felt the way Molly feels . . .

"Do not let your hearts be troubled. Trust in God."

John 14:1a

Alone, Dark, and Quiet

Water poured into the washing machine. The dryer breathed soft, warm air. Molly crawled under the steps next to the laundry room. Sometimes Drew and Lucas took her into this space. It was their hiding place. They kept a flashlight, pillows, and a Bible story-book there. Lucas always let Molly choose the picture, then he'd tell the story. At the end of each story, he'd switch on the flashlight and say, "Jesus is the light of the world." Then Drew and Molly would clap as the light shone in the dark corners.

Molly opened the Bible storybook to the picture of Jesus making a home in heaven. She wondered if Mom Tessa had a room in the big castle. Did her mother know the light of Jesus that led people to his house in heaven?

"I have peanut butter sandwiches," called a voice. It was Drew.

Molly held herself still. Did Drew know what had happened to her mother?

"Are you in here?" Drew crawled into the space with a tray of food.

"I can't find my mother," said Molly.

"She's upstairs talking on the phone. I just came home."

Molly shook her head. "No, my other mother. She died when I wasn't there. Now I don't know if she found her way to Jesus in heaven."

"Let's go ask Mom," Drew said. "She'll know."

I Wonder . . .

I wonder if you know and love someone who is in heaven with Jesus . . .

"There are many rooms in my Father's house."

John 14:2a

Messages

Molly and Drew hurried upstairs. Mom Barna was still on the phone. Molly and Drew sat around the corner from the telephone and listened.

"Yes, Tessa came to Credo Canyon Church looking for a family to take care of her baby. She had just found out she had AIDS."

Drew motioned Molly to follow him into the family room. "It isn't good to have AIDS," he said.

"No," Molly said. "It makes you die."

"We should check at the church," Drew said. "Someone there might know more about your mother."

"Okay."

Drew dressed in his coat and boots. Then he helped Molly put on her things too.

The sun was melting the snow on the sidewalks and streets. But in most places Drew's boots left a footprint, so Molly stepped in the slushy spots that Drew left behind.

Across from the Credo Canyon Church, they waited for the walk signal. "It looks very quiet over there," Molly said. "Quiet makes me feel alone."

Drew took her hand when the signal changed to walk. "Sometimes quiet is good," Drew said. "It makes you listen."

"I'll listen for my mother," Molly said.

I Wonder . . .
I wonder who Jesus has given to you so you aren't alone . . .

"I will not leave you like children who don't have parents. I will come to you."

John 14:18

Credo Canyon Church

Molly and Drew climbed the steps to the front door of the church. Drew pushed against the latch and pulled on the door. It opened, and they walked inside.

Silently Molly followed Drew to the front. "I like it best when the people are here," she said.

When they got to the front, Drew sat on the bench. Molly sat next to him.

"There's a story in the Bible about a girl who died," Drew said. "But Jesus told her to get up."

"And did she?" Molly asked.

"Yep," Drew said. "Got up and walked around just because Jesus said so."

Molly swung her legs and looked around the church. "Jesus can do anything. Even take Mom Tessa to heaven. 'Cept how can I know if he did?"

The sound of a door opening and closing made them scoot next to each other.

"Who's here?" called a voice. "Hello." Then there were footsteps.

"Molly and Drew Barna! What are you doing here?" It was Mrs. Merton, the church secretary.

"I—I'm trying to find out what happened to Mom Tessa," Molly said.

I Wonder . . .
I wonder why Molly likes church best when the people are there . . .

"I will ask the Father. And he will give you another Friend to help you and to be with you forever. The Friend is the Spirit of truth."

John 4:16-17a

Tessa's Wish

Mrs. Merton put her arms around Molly. "I remember a special day about three-and-a-half years ago," Mrs. Merton said. "It was the day your mother came to my office. She carried you in her arms. You were the cutest thing."

"Why did she bring me here?"

Mrs. Merton lifted her hands and clapped them. "It was a wonderful reason. I almost forgot about it. Turn around."

As Molly faced the back of the church, she saw a beautiful colored window at the very top of the church wall. The sunlight from outside shone light all around the picture of Jesus, who had his hands raised up. He was going into the clouds, and his disciples stood on the ground watching.

"Your mother sang in a choir when she was a teenager. Her choir came to Credo Canyon Church for a special program. After she found out she was sick, she remembered this window. Then she decided she wanted her baby to grow up knowing about the window."

Molly moved her hand through the sunbeams that shone through the window. If her mother wanted her to know about Jesus going to heaven, then her mother knew too.

I Wonder . . .
I wonder what reminds you of Jesus' love and peace . . .

"I leave my peace with you. I give my peace to you. I do not give it to you as the world does. Do not let your hearts be troubled. And do not be afraid."

John 14:27

Jesus Turns Water into Wine

John 2:1-11

Has anyone ever reached behind your ear and pulled out a quarter? "Magic," they might have said. Do you know where that quarter came from?

In a magic trick the trickster uses a real object and tries to make you think he is doing something impossible with it. But sooner or later you can find a way to explain it.

What about Jesus' miracles? When he turned water into wine, he used something real and seemed to change it. Or did he *really* change it? A miracle has only one explanation—God.

Song for the Week:
"My God Is So Great," *Songs for LiFE* 35

Prayer for the Week:
Wow! Jesus, you are great!
You are strong and mighty.
We are surprised at what can happen
when you take over.
Thank you for the times when you
    surprise us with your great power.
You can change anything you made.
Change me too. Change me to be
    always praising you. Amen.

Grown-Up Wishes

Trevor and Peter were on their way home from school. They caught snowflakes on their tongues.

"Did you tell Mrs. Page what you want to be for career day?" Trevor asked Peter.

"Nope," Peter said. "I don't know yet. Do you know?"

Trevor reached his tongue out for a big, fluffy flake. "Nope, I don't know either. But it's going to be something important. Maybe a fireman or a policeman."

"How about a paramedic?" Peter asked. "My uncle is a paramedic. He tells exciting stories, and right in the middle of a story, he pulls a quarter out from behind my ear. It surprises me every time because I'm so busy listening to his story."

"Yeah, that'd be cool," Trevor said. "I watch a paramedic show on TV. It'd be great to be a hero and save lives."

The snowflakes doubled, then tripled in number. Trevor and Peter lifted their faces to the sky and let the snow collect on them.

"Help. Someone help!"

Trevor blinked his eyelashes through the snowy layer. He saw Corey Kemp, a sixth grader, running down the sidewalk toward them. He was waving his arms through the white.

"Mr. Ingel needs help!" he shouted at Trevor and Peter.

I Wonder...
I wonder how Corey's cry for help made Trevor and Peter feel...

I also pray that your mind might see more clearly. Then you will know the hope God has chosen you to receive.

Ephesians 1:18a

Call and Pray

"Mr. Ingel is . . . " Corey caught his breath, "trapped under his car. He needs help."

Trevor looked at Peter. "Think fast. What would a paramedic do?"

"I don't know," Peter said. "But I'm calling 911." He ran across the street to the Henry's house.

Trevor followed Corey to the Ingel's driveway. Mr. Ingel was on the ground. His leg was trapped under the back tire. Trevor sat down on the driveway so that he was close to Mr. Ingel.

"I slipped," Mr. Ingel said with short breaths.

Trevor took off his mittens and touched Mr. Ingel's face. Then he wiggled out of his jacket and put it between the icy driveway and Mr. Ingel's face.

"Peter is calling 911," Trevor said. "Are you going to be okay?"

"Yes, Trevor," Mr. Ingel said in a tiny voice, "now that you boys are here."

Trevor wished that was true. But what could they really do? A real paramedic might not even be able to get the car off of Mr. Ingel. "Pray for strength," he told himself. Strength for what, though—strength for Mr. Ingel to stay alive?

Mr. Ingel's eyes closed. "Are you okay?" Peter asked again. This time there was no answer.

I Wonder . . .

I wonder if God always knows when one of his people is hurt . . .

> You will know that the things God's people will receive are rich and glorious.
>
> *Ephesians 1: 18b*

On the Count of Three

Peter came running back. "The paramedics are on their way," he said.
"If only we could lift the car off his leg right now," Corey said.
Trevor jumped up. "Let's try."
"It's impossible," Peter said.

But Trevor and Corey didn't hear Peter. They had their hands under the car's bumper. And in a second Joshua and Caleb Henry were there, too, ready to lift.

"Wake up, Mr. Ingel," Trevor called. "Move your leg when we lift the car."

"One, two, three." Corey counted. "Up."

Trevor didn't think about the weight of the car. He didn't think about how he was smaller than all of his friends. All he thought about was the car coming off of Mr. Ingel's leg. And for a blink of time it did. And at that same moment, Mr. Ingel groaned and moved his leg.

The car touched the ground and Trevor felt the weight under his hands. A weight that could not be budged by his hands even with the help of the others.

Sirens screamed around the corner. Two men hopped out of the back doors and wheeled a stretcher over to Mr. Ingel. "Looks like a broken leg," said the man with sandy-colored hair. "By the way, how did you get the car off of him?"

Trevor, Peter, and Corey looked at each other. They didn't know how to answer.

I Wonder . . .
I wonder if you know the answer to the man's question . . .

And you will know his great power.

Ephesians 1:19a

The Right Answer

By the time the paramedics had Mr. Ingel in the back of their van, a large crowd had gathered together on Stepping Stone Avenue.

The sandy-haired paramedic poked his head out of the back door. "The gentlemen is asking for three young men. Is it possible for Trevor, Peter, and Corey to ride to the hospital with us?"

Mrs. Tamiko and Mrs. Wit agreed that would be fine, and they promised to tell Corey's mother what happened too.

"My name is Mike," said the paramedic. "And this is my helper, Tom. Now who was the young man who called us to say a car was on top of a man?"

"That'd be me," Peter said.

"Good thinking to call us," Mike said. "But now can you explain who got the car off of him."

"We're not sure how we did it," Corey said.

Trevor thought about the people who were heroes in rescue stories. This could be his chance to come out looking like one of those heroes. But he didn't feel like a hero. There was no way to explain how he felt except to say that God gave him strength.

"It was God," Trevor whispered. "After Mr. Ingel moved his leg. We couldn't lift the car again. Not for all the money in the world."

I Wonder . . .
I wonder if you've ever had a chance to tell someone about God's power . . .

> It [God's power] can't be compared with anything else.
>
> *Ephesians 1:19b*

The Final Report

The boys sat in the waiting room while they wheeled Mr. Ingel to X ray. Before Trevor could open the sports magazine to the soccer article, a crew of cameramen and reporters surrounded them.

"Are you the young boys who rescued Mr. Ingel?" A microphone was shoved in front of Trevor.

"We were walking home from school when Corey called to us."

A pony-tailed man moved the microphone over to Corey. "Can you tell us what happened?"

"Mr. Ingel was scraping the snow off his car's windshield when the car rolled backwards. It knocked him down, and his leg got trapped. I saw it, so I called for help."

"And just a few kids responded," said the reporter to the camera, but together they were able to lift the car off Mr. Ingel's leg.

"That was some rush of adrenaline," said another reporter.

"I didn't think kids had that power in them."

Trevor thought about when he felt his body going into high gear during a soccer game. No, this wasn't the same.

"It wasn't our power," Trevor said. "It was God working through us."

Twenty flashes seemed to go off when Trevor said that. And suddenly it felt as if he had told the whole world.

I Wonder . . .
I wonder if Trevor's words helped others believe in God's power . . .

It [God's power] is at work for us who believe.

Ephesians 1: 19c

Jesus Feeds Four Thousand People

Matthew 15:29-39

Do you like incredible stories? Stories that are almost impossible to believe?

The story of Jesus feeding four thousand people is one of those kinds of stories.

Perhaps you think miracles like that only could happen when Jesus was on earth. But there are incredible stories about what happens in our world because of Jesus today too. And sometimes they are about people being fed. The most amazing thing about these stories is that people like you are the source of the food. Just like the seven loaves and few fish that the disciples had were the source of food for four thousand people. Giving a little has a way of multiplying.

Song for the Week:
"There's a Spirit in the Air,"
Songs for LiFE 192

Prayer for the Week:
Jesus, how can the little that I have
help others?
Show me how to give so that
there is plenty for everyone.
Thank you for caring about the hungry.
Help me to care too. Amen.

Greatness

Peter unfolded a *National Geographic* map of the world. He hopped with his fingers from one country to the next.

"I want to go here, and here, and here," he said. "Just like Andy Ingel."

"Wow!" Trevor said. "What does Andy do?"

"He's a pilot," Peter said. "He delivers supplies to missionaries in Africa."

Trevor scooted across the floor closer to the map. He zoomed his finger from the United States to Africa. "I'd like to know more about the jungles and people in Africa," he said.

"You can ask Andy tonight. Mrs. Ingel invited us," Peter said. "Andy came home to see his dad because of the accident. Last time he was home he told about how God saved him from a snake."

Trevor had never met Andy. It sounded like his work was exciting and dangerous. It would take a brave person to go into the wild jungles. Trevor could almost see a tall, young, husky version of Mr. Ingel rolling up his sleeve to show a long, jagged scar.

"Andy says he'll never give up," Peter said. "That's why I think he's so brave and why I want to be like him."

Trevor nodded. One thing for sure, he was going to the Ingels' tonight to meet Andy and see if he was as brave as Peter said.

I Wonder . . .
I wonder what faraway places you'd like to travel to . . .

I wonder what faraway people you'd like to meet . . .

Without a Home or Country

"Trevor and Peter! Welcome," Mrs. Ingel said. "Andy is eager to meet the boys who helped rescue his dad. Corey Kemp and the Henry boys are here too."

They followed Mrs. Ingel into the family room where Mr. Ingel was resting.

A young man with fine blond hair stood up when they came into the room. He held out his hand to Trevor. "You must be the boy who got my dad to move his leg when the car was lifted. It's Trevor, right? I'm Andy Ingel."

Trevor nodded. He ducked behind Peter. What could he say to this person? According to Peter, Andy was supposed to be a brave hero, but he looked very ordinary.

While Peter talked to Andy, Trevor escaped to the sofa where Corey, Josh, and Caleb were passing around pictures.

Trevor held out his hand for a stack of pictures. The first picture showed a group of dark-skinned kids standing and sitting around a shabby tent. They wore strips of rags for clothes.

Andy came over to them. "These children had to leave their home in Rwanda because of wars and fighting. Many of them were separated from their parents. They lived in tents with two adults who were willing to take care of them. Since they had to leave home so quickly, they couldn't bring food, blankets, or toys."

Trevor wasn't sure he would even touch these kids. Did Andy help them?

I Wonder . . .
I wonder how the children in Rwanda felt while they were waiting for food and blankets . . .

When you suffer, be patient.

Romans 12:12b

Food for Thousands

T revor flipped over to the next picture. Three boys were grinning. One boy was biting into a raw potato.

"They ate them like apples," Andy said. "Potatoes were considered a treat."

The next picture showed girls tossing a ball.

"The balls we brought them were popular," Andy said. "But in the next picture you'll see unhappy faces. Medical teams had to give shots so everyone could stay healthy. Since there were no bathrooms and running water, there were many ways to get sick."

The line for getting a shot zigzagged far in the distance. More pictures showed men working on roads and digging holes.

"See those tools," Andy said. "People in the United States and Canada were praying for the people of Rwanda. Many sent money. For every $4.10 they sent, we could buy a tool for a man. Then he'd go to work and earn food for his whole family."

"You mean a four-dollar tool could be used to feed a family every day?" Peter asked.

"That's right," Andy said. "All I did was deliver those tools. Between food and supplies, we helped 300,000 people in Rwanda."

I Wonder . . .
I wonder how many ways you can think of to help people in countries like Rwanda . . .

Cambodia

Mrs. Ingel came into the room with bowls of buttery popcorn. She had a large bowl and a tall glass of juice for each boy. When it came to popcorn, Trevor had no trouble finishing off a large bowl.

"Are you going back to Africa?" Peter asked.

"I've spent the past three years in Africa," Andy said. "It's a place I love very much. The people are in my heart and prayers every day. But last month I went to Cambodia for a short time. Now I must decide what to do next."

"Are people running away from wars there too?" Trevor asked.

"No," Andy said, "but thousands of people have lost legs, arms, and hands in a previous war. This makes it hard for parents to take care of their children. The children were never given vaccinations for polio. Now many of them are crippled."

Trevor slowly munched on his popcorn. What would he do if he were Andy? He watched Andy stir around the leftover kernels in the popcorn bowl. Andy seemed to be miles away.

Then he started another story. "One evening as my friend was finishing a bowl of rice, a ten-year-old girl begged for his last bit of rice. She wanted it for her two brothers, a six-year-old and a baby. Their mother had died. Their father had run away with another woman. They lived with their grandmother, but she was ill."

I Wonder . . .

I wonder where you would go if you were Andy . . .

I wonder why you'd make that choice . . .

Share with God's people who are in need.

Romans 12:13a

More Than a Bag of Rice

Be joyful with those who are joyful.

Romans 12:15a

Trevor cracked a corn kernel between his teeth. He had eaten enough popcorn to make him more than full, but the half-popped kernels were fun to crack. He always had more than enough of everything. Even if he shared some of it, he'd still have plenty.

"I know what you should do," Trevor said. "Go to Cambodia and take along bags of rice. We have fifty-pound bags at the restaurant. I'm sure you could have a couple."

"I like your big heart," Andy said.

Trevor pictured the girl having a bowl for herself and one for each of her brothers.

"How many pounds of rice do you use in a week at the restaurant?" Andy asked.

"I'm not sure. Probably a hundred pounds or more."

"And how many people does that feed?"

Trevor didn't think Andy was interested in the restaurant business. Why was he asking all these questions? Then Trevor thought of Andy's story from Africa. What the people really needed was a way to earn their own food.

"You don't need food, do you?" Trevor said.

"In the beginning, yes," Andy said, "but the people in Cambodia will be better off when they can grow the rice for themselves."

"I'd like to give you money," Trevor said, "to help the Cambodians get started." This time he pictured hundreds of girls and boys in a field of rice.

I Wonder . . .
I wonder what you would like to have happen to people in Cambodia or Rwanda . . .

I wonder if there's something you could do today for them . . .

Be sure to check page 248 for more of the story.

Jesus Heals a Man Who Can't See

Mark 8:22-30

I n this week's story some people brought a man who couldn't see to Jesus. Then they begged Jesus to heal the man.

Have you ever prayed, even begged Jesus to heal someone?

Maybe you have and you were disappointed. The person you prayed for wasn't fixed up as quickly as you expected. Or this person had to go to the doctor more than once before he or she got better.

Look again at Jesus and the blind man. Jesus didn't make the blind man see perfectly the first time. The Bible doesn't tell us why. But it does tell us that Jesus stayed with the man until the people in the man's sight no longer looked like walking trees.

Song for the Week:
"Let Me Be Your Servant, Jesus," *Songs for LiFE* 244

Prayer for the Week:
Jesus, there are many people who need you.
Help me pay attention so I know who they are.
Then remind me to bring them to you.
Right now I want to pray for _____.
And Jesus, please stay with them.
And stay with me, so I can be like you. Amen.

Sugar for Grandpa Ingel

"Come in, Sugar," Grandma Ingel said, opening the door to her only grandchild, Janell. "I'm glad your dad could drop you off on his way to the office. Grandpa needs a little 'sugar' today."

Janell hugged her Grandma. She knew Grandma would call her "Sugar" and say Grandpa needed some of that sweetness. That was Grandma's way.

"Did you bring your schoolbooks?" Grandma asked.

Janell slid the backpack off her shoulders. "Not today. Mom says I'm far enough ahead that I can skip a day. That's a good part of being home-schooled."

She took her favorite storybooks out of her backpack. "I'll read to Grandpa if we run out of things to talk about."

"I'm sure Grandpa would like that," Grandma said. "You are getting to be a good reader."

Grandma went to her sewing room downstairs. Janell tiptoed into the family room where a bed had been set up for Grandpa. She could see that his eyes were closed. His broken leg was propped up on the pillows. She tapped the hard white cast. Everything about Grandpa was white. His hair, his face, and the big fat leg. Janell never noticed Grandpa being so white before. It was scary to see Grandpa so white.

Grandpa always said God was good to him. Would he still say that?

I Wonder . . .
I wonder if Grandpa Ingel would still say God is good . . .

Grandpa's Prayer Book

Grandpa opened one eye. Then he opened the other one too. "I was just dreaming about you," he said to Janell, "and hoping you'd come today."

"I've been asking God to make you better, Grandpa," Janell said. "When is it going to happen?"

Grandpa Ingel shifted in his bed so he could sit up. "Let's look at my prayer book," he said. He reached for a brown leather loose-leaf notebook from the end table.

Janell sat on the edge of the bed beside him. She watched as he turned the pages. "Why do you call it your prayer book? It looks like newspaper articles and letters."

"In a way it is," Grandpa said. "These are prayer letters and newsletters from missionaries and Christian doctors all over the world."

"Oh, Grandpa, what's the matter with that girl in the picture?"

"That's Rosita. The right side of her face is twice the size it should be because she was born with an unusual growth. Other children made fun of her. They called her names. Even her own family didn't treat her well. Her father sent her out to the streets to beg. He knew some people would feel sorry for her and give her money. Then he'd take the money to buy beer for himself."

"I'm glad she's in your prayer book, Grandpa, but can't something else be done for her?"

I Wonder . . .
I wonder what God can do for someone like Rosita . . .

He forgives all my sins. He heals my sicknesses.

Psalm 103:3

Who Will Help?

"Rosita lived in a small village in Honduras, far away from any doctors."

"Jesus should go there," Janell said. "When he was on earth he healed all kinds of sicknesses. Remember the blind man? Jesus made him well without any doctors."

"That's right," Grandpa Ingel said. "And Jesus did go to Honduras."

Janell's eyes opened wide.

"Jesus went through the love of some very special people," Grandpa said. "A group of doctors went to Honduras so they could give the people medical help. When they looked at the growth on Rosita's face, they had to say no. It was too tricky to operate on Rosita. Maybe they could do it if it was in the United States where they had special equipment and clean hospitals. But not in Honduras."

Janell snuggled against Grandpa. "I wish she could come to our hospital."

"One of the doctors wished he could bring her to the United States too," Grandpa said. "So he got busy asking people to help Rosita. One group paid for the trip to the United States and for the operation. Then a family opened their home so she'd have a place to stay before and after the operation."

"Did the operation work?" Janell asked.

Grandpa turned the page of the newsletter. And there was Rosita with the same dark skin and big brown eyes. But now both cheeks were the same size.

I Wonder . . .

I wonder how Rosita and the blind man are alike . . .

Happy Eyes

"It's not just her cheeks," Janell said. "Her eyes are different. They don't look like they are staring. She has happy eyes."

"You're right." Grandpa said. "Let me tell you the rest of her story. The operation lasted five hours. She lost a lot of blood, so the doctors had to use blood donated by other people. It was a successful operation, though. Soon she was able to leave the hospital and live with her American family. They sent her to school. It was the first time Rosita had been taught how to read and write."

"How old was she?" Janell asked.

"Nine years old," Grandpa said.

Janell looked at Rosita's smiling face again. Now she knew two reasons why Rosita's face had changed.

"There's more," Grandpa said. "Rosita wasn't used to being loved or hugged. She didn't know how to act when the family hugged her."

Janell kissed Grandpa's cheek. "I can't imagine not having hugs or kisses."

"Me either," Grandpa said. "But Rosita learned. After a while she'd pull up a chair behind the mother of the family and give her a tight hug."

"Love and hugs are what everyone should have," Janell said.

I Wonder . . .

I wonder what good things you have . . . and if they make you feel full of life . . .

He satisfies me with the good things I long for. Then I feel young again, just like an eagle.

Psalm 103:5

Never an End

"**D**id Rosita stay in America?" Janell asked.

"No," Grandpa said. "There never was a plan to keep her—just to help her. She still loved her brothers and sisters in Honduras. After four months in America, she returned to Honduras at Christmas. She brought gifts home for her family. She also had two new outfits of clothing so that she could go to school."

"What about her dad?" Janell asked. "Did he treat her right?"

"Many people were worried about that. Soon after she went home, some Christians in Honduras asked her father for permission to bring her to live with another family. Now she goes to a Christian school in Honduras. She loves to sing about Jesus."

Janell looked at both pictures of Rosita again. Grandpa was right. Jesus was in Honduras. No one loved Rosita until the people who loved Jesus met her. She was healed because many people loved Jesus. There wasn't an end to good things for Rosita.

She turned the page in Grandpa's prayer book. There were more stories and more people who were healed because of those who loved Jesus.

"Are you worried about your leg, Grandpa?"

"No. It hurts a little right now, but it's sort of nice being like the blind man and Rosita. You and everyone I know is asking Jesus to heal me. I get to know the love of Jesus through the love of others."

I Wonder . . .
I wonder how you can show the love of Jesus to someone today . . .

The LORD does what is right and fair for all those who are beaten down.

Psalm 103:6

Be sure to check page 249 for more of the story.

The Good Shepherd

Matthew 18:12-13; John 10:1-18

Imagine if everywhere you went—at the store, at the library, at the park—people knew your name. And as soon as they saw you, they'd wave and run up to you, wanting to know how you were doing.

Of course this happens to famous people. But in a way it can happen to you too. Because no matter where you are, Jesus knows you. He knows what you are doing, and he doesn't get you mixed up with anyone else. He wants you to know that he is the Good Shepherd—the one who knows his sheep by name.

Song for the Week:
"The Lord, My Shepherd,"
   Songs for LiFE 201, stanzas 1 & 5

Prayer for the Week:
Jesus, I like to say your name.
Your name is like a family name,
because you know me like
I'm part of your family.
Thank you. Amen.

Water

Tabitha Fransico looped her jacket sleeves around her waist. She took a deep breath of the air that made the icicles drip, drop, plop. Yesterday the sky had been black with clouds, and the wind had whipped around corners. But today the clouds and wind were gone, leaving the sun to do its work.

When she came to Thistle Lane, Tabitha saw a stream of water rushing against the curb. She thought she could jump over the water. But she didn't make it. Her left foot landed in the dark water, and the stream swept the black slip-on shoe off her foot. Tabitha hopped onto the sidewalk as her shoe floated away.

"Did you lose something?"

Tabitha turned around. There was Joshua Henry laughing at her. "My shoe."

Josh ran along the curb until he caught up with the floating shoe. He ran back to Tabitha with the dripping shoe.

"Good thing you aren't in the big flood," he said.

She grabbed the shoe from him and ran home. That Josh was such a pain, making it seem like nothing serious had happened to her.

Grandma was waiting for her at the door with a pair of fuzzy slippers. "I saw what happened," she said, giving her granddaughter a hug.

Tabitha pulled off her stockings and wiggled her toes into the warm furry insides.

I Wonder . . .

I wonder why Tabitha thought Josh didn't care about what happened . . .

I wonder if Tabitha might be wrong . . .

The LORD is my shepherd. He gives me everything I need.

Psalm 23:1

The Newspaper Picture

"Grandma, is there a big flood?"

"Yes, parts of Texas had twenty inches of rain in thirty-six hours. In some places the rivers have filled the streets and yards, and have poured into the houses and buildings."

Tabitha sipped the hot chocolate that Grandma had brought her. Josh was right. A little stream in the street was nothing.

"What do people do when the water comes into their house?" Tabitha asked.

"Mostly they have to leave. There is an article in the paper. Some pictures too."

Tabitha got off of her comfortable spot on the sofa. She went into the kitchen and sat by the table to read the paper. There it was on the front page—water filling a street as if it were a river. Two girls about her age sat on top of a truck cab with the water only a few inches from their toes.

Underneath the picture it identified the two girls as twins—LaReina and LeNora Ramirez. Everything about them was the same—their long black hair and their sad eyes. Tabitha pulled the scrunchie out of her long black hair. Her hair was the same color as LaReina's and LeNora's.

Did they lose more than their shoes? Tabitha had her grandma to take care of her, but who was taking care of LaReina and LeNora? It looked like they were all alone. Tabitha had to think of a way to help them.

I Wonder . . .
I wonder if you always know that someone cares about you . . .

He gives me new strength.

Psalm 23:3a

The Quilt

Tabitha thought about the money in her lamb bank. No, there wasn't enough. She had spent most of it at Christmastime. She thought about doing extra chores for Grandma. No, Grandma had to be very careful to make the money come out right at the end of the month. And working for a neighbor wouldn't be good either. Grandma got lonely while Tabitha was at school. They only had each other for family, and that made them more important to each other.

Tabitha padded back to the living room in her fluffy yellow feet. Grandma was bent over the quilt frame, making tiny stitches.

"This is your prettiest quilt yet," Tabitha said. "The dark rose and green are my favorite colors."

Grandma was so quiet Tabitha could hear the needle poking through the fabric.

"The paper said the shelters need blankets for the flood victims," Tabitha said.

"I know," Grandma said. "I've been thinking about that. Pastor Lenci is taking a load of donations down tomorrow morning."

This time Tabitha was very quiet. She touched the tiny stitches around a rose-flowered square. Finally she spoke. "Are you thinking what I'm thinking?"

"You know I am," Grandma said. "If you fix supper, I can finish the quilt tonight."

I Wonder . . .
I wonder how Tabitha and Grandma had the same idea . . .

Three Girls in a Flood

After they finished their supper of soup and sandwiches, Tabitha started her homework. Multiplication was easy for Tabitha, but tonight 3 x 4 didn't make sense. She closed her eyes. Her mind jumped to the picture of LaReina and LeNora. The water in the picture started moving fast. It carried LaReina and LeNora away just like the water carried Tabitha's shoe. Then the water picked up Tabitha too. It carried her away from Grandma and her house. The water carried her away to where it was black—blacker than a night without moon or stars.

Tabitha opened her eyes and shivered. What if LaReina and LeNora didn't get the new quilt? What if they were carried away by the water and never made it to a shelter?

She ripped a page out of her math notebook. With her pencil she wrote: "This quilt is for LaReina and LeNora Ramirez. They are the girls in the picture. Please find them. Love, Tabitha Fransico."

"Grandma, may I pin this note and the picture of LaReina and LeNora to the quilt?"

Grandma read the note. "I don't know, honey. The shelter is full of people who have lost their homes and all their possessions. We don't know if Pastor Lenci is going to the same shelter as the Ramirezes."

"That's why we need the note. I know Pastor Lenci will try to find them if we ask."

Grandma hugged Tabitha. "Yes, he'll try if it's possible."

I Wonder . . .

I wonder if God smiles on us when we try to help people in trouble . . .

> Even though I walk through the darkest valley, I will not be afraid.
>
> *Psalm 23:4a*

The Call

You are with me.
Your shepherd's
rod and staff
comfort me.

Psalm 23:4b

At school Mrs. Love's third-grade class talked about helping flood victims.

"We gave one of my Grandma's special quilts," Tabitha said.

"Blockhead," Jeremy said. "They need food, money, water pumps and medicines. I heard it on the radio."

"The paper said blankets," Tabitha said.

"Old blankets," Jeremy said. "Just something to keep them warm. You could have sold the quilt and made lots of money."

"I'm sure Tabitha did what she thought was best," Mrs. Love said. "End of discussion. Turn in your math homework."

Tabitha turned in her unfinished worksheet and put her head in her hands.

After school Tabitha pretended to clean out her desk so she wouldn't have to leave with the others. When the classroom cleared out, she got her things and left by herself.

Grandma stood on the porch waving to her as she dragged her feet toward home.

"Hurry, Tabitha," Grandma yelled. "There's a phone call for you."

Tabitha took the phone that Grandma handed her. "Tabitha," said a small voice, "this is LaReina."

Another voice jumped in. "And LeNora. We want to thank you for the quilt. It's the best thing that has happened to us—ever. Thank you."

I Wonder . . .
I wonder if God has ever surprised you through the caring acts of other people . . .

Jesus Blesses the Children

Mark 10:13-16

If a friend listens to your problem, the problem can seem smaller.

"It'll be okay," he says. "I'll help you."

If a friend listens to your good news, the good news seems bigger.

"Wow," she says. "That is exciting."

When Jesus was on earth, his words and touches healed and encouraged many people.

The children who came to Jesus one day were told not to bother Jesus. But Jesus wanted the children to come. He welcomed them with open arms. Now they knew, and all children can know, that Jesus is excited about blessing them. He makes your biggest problems grow smaller and your best work grow bigger.

Song for the Week:

"It Makes No Difference," *Songs for LiFE* 206, stanzas 1, 2, 3, and the following stanza:

> "It makes no difference how old we are.
> Jesus hears the young and old."

> *Chorus*

Prayer for the Week:

> Jesus, I want to run right up to you
> because I know you won't send me away.
> I know you will look at me,
> and say "I hear you, I love you."
> Jesus, thank you. I love you too. Amen.

Bulletin Board News

On Wednesday evening, Josh Henry hurried to his boys' club activity room in Credo Canyon Church. Tonight they were starting a new project—a birdhouse. He heard voices coming from the room. Peter Wit and Trevor Tamiko!

Josh had hoped he'd be the first one tonight. Woodworking was his best hobby. And with a head start from the leader, he could do as well as Peter and Trevor.

He checked his watch—6:40—twenty minutes before the meeting started. Peter and Trevor did everything together—even coming early. It was no wonder they always had the best projects.

He leaned against the bulletin board in the hallway, wishing for a friend who would help him and work with him like Peter and Trevor worked together.

"Isn't that a great story about the Ramirez family?"

He spun around. Tabitha Fransico. Where did she come from?

She pointed to a picture on the bulletin board. "That's Paco, LaReina, LeNora, Huey, and little Humblelina. Pastor Lenci said they might move to Credo Canyon."

"How old is Paco?" Josh asked.

"He's in fourth grade," Tabitha said. "So I'd guess he's your age."

"Cool," Josh said. "Paco'd probably like someone to show him around."

I Wonder . . .
I wonder if you ever wish for a really good friend like Josh did . . .

And God is able to shower all kinds of blessings on you.

2 Corinthians 9:8a

An Idea

"Where would they live if they moved here?" Josh asked.

"In the apartments," Tabitha said. "If Pastor Lenci can rent one."

"Yippee!" Josh shouted.

"It might not happen," Tabitha said. "There are some regulars against it."

"Regulars?" Josh asked. "Do you mean regulations?"

"Yes, that's it," Tabitha said. "No more than four people in a two-bedroom apartment."

Josh pushed his glasses up on his nose. He counted the Ramirezes. Two parents and five kids. That was as many as the Barna's family. And even with a large house, the Barnas filled their space.

"It'll never happen," Josh said.

Tabitha sniffed. "Don't you think LaReina and LeNora could be my sisters?"

Josh liked Tabitha's long black hair. He liked her brown eyes that reminded him of the middle of sunflowers even in the wintertime. And he liked to tease her, even though it made her angry at him. Yes, the girls in the picture had hair and eyes almost the same as Tabitha. They would make good friends for her.

Then Josh had an idea. "Meet me in the fort after school tomorrow," Josh said.

I Wonder . . .

I wonder if Josh and Tabitha can do anything to bring the Ramirezes to Credo Canyon . . . or if only adults can make it happen . . .

> In all things and at all times you will have everything you need.
>
> *2 Corinthians 9:8b*

An Unwanted House

After school on Thursday Josh took a hammer out of the garage. He pounded the nails on the boards that led up the tree to his fort. If Tabitha was going to climb up into his fort, he didn't want any loose boards.

He had thought about inviting her a couple of other times. But then another thought would stop him: Peter and Trevor wouldn't invite a girl—especially not a third-grade one.

At 3:42, he saw her coming.

"Up here," he called. "Climb up the boards like a ladder."

It didn't take her long. She didn't seem one bit afraid.

"Wow!" she said. "You can see a long way from up here. And you can see right into my backyard. You don't spy on me, do you, Joshua Henry?"

Josh could feel himself turning red right up to the tips of his ears. "Do you see the house next to yours?"

"Yeah," Tabitha said. "It's a mess. Grandma said those people didn't pay their rent. Then when the owner told them to get out, they made holes in the walls."

"I've been inside," Josh said. "There's a window that's unlocked in the cellar."

Tabitha's eyes grew big. "Is it spooky?"

"It's full of garbage. But if someone bought it, fixed it up, and let the Ramirezes live there, it would be better than an empty house."

I Wonder . . .

I wonder if Jesus ever helps you think of good things to do for others . . .

Not a No

"Kids like us can't buy houses," Tabitha said. "Even if we had the money."

"Do you want to give up finding a place for the Ramirezes?"

"Guess not." Tabitha straightened out the little rug that Josh had by the front opening. "You could call the number on the For Sale sign," she said.

They scrambled down the tree ladder. The late winter sky turned dark gray as they ran through Tabitha's backyard and around to the front of 1820 Rimrock Avenue.

Josh said the phone number over several times until he was sure he had it memorized. Then they agreed to meet again tomorrow after school.

When Josh got home, he dialed the number. As soon as it rang, he pushed the off button. What could he say—that he was nine years old and he wanted to buy a house? He closed his eyes to pray; then he dialed again.

"Home Estate Real Estate. Ann Brody," said a voice.

Josh lowered his chin into his neck to make his voice deeper. "How cheap would you sell the house at 1820 Rimrock? There's a family who lost their home in a flood."

"Well, it is a fixer-upper," said the woman. "I'll check with the owner. Give me your number. I'll call you back."

Josh gave her the information, then he let the phone fall into his lap. She didn't say no. She said she'd check.

I Wonder . . .
I wonder if the owner of the house has a generous heart . . .

God will also supply and increase.

2 Corinthians 9:10b

A Wanted House

Josh went to the garage. He put his birdhouse on the workbench, tied a carpenter's belt around his waist, and filled it with nails. Carefully he tapped the little nails that connected the roof to the walls. If Paco was here now, they could build another birdhouse for Paco.

"Please make it so Paco can come," he whispered to God.

"Josh," called his mom. "There's a phone call for you. A Mrs. Brody."

The house! Josh's heart pounded as he reached for the phone.

"Good news," said Ann Brody. "The owner is willing to work with the family. He just needs the details."

Josh told her everything Tabitha had told him. He even told about the quilt.

"We're going to make this work, Josh," said Ann Brody. "By the way, how old are you?"

Josh wondered if his voice could pass for twelve. But if this house worked for the Ramerizes, he might meet Ann Brody. "I turned nine on January 17th," he said.

He heard her chuckle. "Well you're the first nine-year-old client I've had. But perhaps the best. This is an exciting project."

As Josh returned the phone to its cradle he thought of everyone who could help with this house. He would have a partner after all—many partners.

I Wonder . . .

I wonder what partners you could find to reach out to someone in trouble . . .

> He will increase the results of your good works.
>
> *2 Corinthians 9:10c*

The Good Samaritan

Luke 10:25-37

Help set the table. Help your brother clean the garage. Help pick up the trash in the school yard.

You know it's your responsibility to help.

The young man who came to Jesus knew what was expected of him too. But Jesus told the story of the Good Samaritan to show him there was more. Those who are part of God's family must also help because of the love of God in them. The love of God opens your eyes to see people who need help —a boy in Africa who is starving, a girl who has everything money can buy but doesn't know Jesus, a family in South America who has never seen a doctor, an elderly lady living in a nursing home who is lonely, a boy in your class who doesn't have a friend.

Song for the Week:
"Jesu, Jesu, Fill Us with Your Love," *Songs for LiFE* 251

Prayer for the Week:
Jesus, open my eyes so that I can see
what others need.
Fill me with your love so that
I can love with a big heart.
Help me to see your kingdom full
of all kinds of people. Amen.

The Ride

A red sports car was parked outside Josh's house when he came home from school. Josh whistled. Wow, he'd like a ride in that car. Who did it belong to?

A tall, black man dressed in a dark suit, white shirt, and tie walked out of his house with Mrs. Henry. "You must be Josh," he said. "My name is Sam Jasper. I'm the owner of the house at 1820 Rimrock Avenue."

Josh gulped. He was hoping for a small grandfather-type owner. One who just wanted to let a family without a house have a place to live.

"We can make a deal if the Ramirezes can make monthly payments," Sam said.

Josh gulped again. He had no idea if the Ramirezes had any money. "We'd have to talk to Pastor Lenci," he said. "He's met the family. I—I just wanted it to work."

"Let's take care of that now," Sam Jasper said.

Josh nodded. "Pastor Lenci has an office in Credo Canyon Church."

"Hop in," Sam said, opening the car door for Josh.

A few minutes ago he'd thought it'd be awesome speeding away in this car. Now he wasn't sure about anything. He looked for an answer in his mother's face. She smiled an okay to him.

Josh stared at his feet as the car purred away from his house. He had the biggest feet in his class. If only big feet meant he was big enough to make grown-up decisions.

I Wonder...
I wonder if you sometimes feel that your gifts aren't enough to help other people...

The Plan

Sam parked the car in the church lot. "I'll wait here while you talk to Pastor Lenci," he said.

As Josh hopped out of the car, a robin landed in the bare branches of the tree above him. Once before Josh had seen a robin in February. At that time he wondered if a robin would be able to make a home so early in the year. Now he wished no one had to worry about a home—not a robin —not the Ramirezes—not anyone.

It didn't take long to explain the situation to Pastor Lenci.

"Between you and Tabitha," Pastor Lenci said, "you've made things happen for the Ramirezes that never would have happened otherwise. Don Bennett also stepped in when he heard Mr. Ramirez owned a print shop that was wiped out in the flood. And since Don needs help in his print shop, he offered Mr. Ramirez a job."

"So the Ramirezes can make payments to Sam Jasper?"

"Exactly," Pastor Lenci said.

"Then I can make the deal with Sam Jasper!" Josh said.

"And I'll call Mr. Ramirez," said Pastor Lenci, "to tell them to come."

Pastor Lenci reached out to shake Josh's hand. Josh felt the warmth of the large hand. Then he felt small standing there in the pastor's office filled with books and Bibles. He sensed he was part of a greater plan—a plan that was helping the Ramirezes.

I Wonder . . .
I wonder if giving to others ever makes you feel part of a greater plan . . .

You have shown yourselves to be worthy by what you have given.

2 Corinthians 9:13a

The Deal

So people will praise God because you obey him.

2 Corinthians 9:13b

Sam Jasper had a calculator in his hand when Josh returned to the car. That meant big numbers—could there be numbers too big to stop the deal?

"Mr. Ramirez has a job," Josh said as soon as he got into the passenger seat.

Sam's big brown hands clapped the cover shut on the calculator. "Just the news I wanted to hear."

Josh kept his eyes on the calculator. "How much does he need to pay every month?"

A laugh that was more like a roar came out of Sam. "You're quite the businessman," he said. "We're not going to worry about money yet. I'll let them decide what they can afford to pay."

"But the deal. I thought you needed to make enough money."

"Josh," said Sam. "I own many houses, and I drive hard deals to get the rent I want or the best sale price. Then one day Ann Brody calls to tell me about you and what you want. The whole idea surprised me so much, I just decided to take a chance. It has made me think about someone else for a change."

"It didn't bother you that I'm a kid?"

"Nope," Sam said. "That made it better. Besides, no one else had the idea that a run-down house could be put to good use."

I Wonder . . .
I wonder if God used Josh to help someone besides the Ramirez family . . .

— 142 —

Donations

Run-down house. Suddenly Josh remembered the mess inside of the house. He studied the gold rings on Sam's hand. Did he dare ask Sam for more? "I—uh—if it was my house I'd fix it up."

"I figured the Ramirezes could fix it," Sam said. "Then I could turn around and say they bought the house with their work and their money."

"Yeah," Josh said. "That's a great idea. But the Ramirezes might not have hammers or nails. Could my dad and I help?"

Sam opened a notebook with a weekly calendar. "Let's see, today is Thursday. Do you think you could meet me at the house on Saturday? If you could find a team to work on the house, you could give the Ramirezes a head start."

"You bet," Josh said.

After Sam brought Josh home, he ran to tell the good news to Tabitha. It didn't take her long to come up with a plan to spread the news. Within an hour, they got donations from everyone in the neighborhood. Sheetrock from the Sanders, shingles from the Wits, paint from the Mertons, cabinets from the Ingels, sheets and towels from the Barnas, food from the Tamikos, and curtains from the Bennetts.

I Wonder . . .
I wonder why Josh's neighbors were so willing to help . . .

That proves that you really believe the good news about Christ.

2 Corinthians 9:13c

Saturday's Work

On Saturday morning, Josh rode in the pickup with his dad to 1820 Rimrock. They had a new kitchen sink in the back of the pickup.

When they pulled up to the house, Josh decided this was like going to a party. But instead of party hats, he saw paint caps.

As he walked backwards carrying one end of the sink across from his dad, Josh bumped into a boy with shiny, black hair. He wore a brightly colored fitted shirt that was stained and missing several buttons. A cigarette lighter in his hand flicked on and off. Josh was puzzled over this stranger for a second. Then it came to him. This was Paco.

Paco followed Josh and his dad into the kitchen. After they balanced the sink on the counter next to the sink hole, Josh kept a grip on the sink. Paco wasn't what he had expected. He didn't fit the picture Josh had in mind for a best buddy.

"I'm good at working with tools," Paco said. "What can I do?"

Josh let go of the sink. He put his hand over his special hammer in his tool belt. Could he let Paco use his tools? Pounding and sawing noise filled up a silence between them. Then the hammering seemed to chant to him—give, give, giving is good.

The chant went from his ears to his heart.

He held out his hand to Paco. "Welcome to Credo Canyon."

I Wonder . . .
I wonder who can help us accept people who are different from us . . .

Jesus and Two Sisters

Luke 10:38-42

Close your eyes—picture your best friend. Do you know your friend's favorite flavor of ice cream? What about a favorite book or movie? Do you know your friend's middle name?

If you know these things about your friend, it's probably because you've spent time together.

Mary wanted to spend time with Jesus—they were friends. You can spend time with him too—in church, in prayer, and when you read his letters to you, the Bible.

Song for the Week:

"Jesus Is a Friend of Mine," *Songs for LiFE* 36

Prayer for the Week:

Jesus, my friend, you are the best.
Every day and every hour
you are there for me.
Thank you for the Bible,
and for all the ways
I can know you.
I praise you for being
   my Savior. Amen.

LaReina and LeNora

We worship God by the power of his Spirit.

Philippians 3:3b

LeNora refolded her sweater and put it between her head and the car window. All night long they had been riding in Grandfather Pappy's old Buick.

Mama had told them to sleep. But LeNora didn't sleep. Whenever she closed her eyes, the car turned into a raft floating down a river of muddy water instead of a car moving along the forever gray stretch of highway. She pressed her flashlight button to make sure the battery wasn't dead.

LaReina was tucked under the quilt from the Credo Canyon girl, Tabitha. Huey and Humblelina were under the quilt too. Mama kept Pappy awake.

Papa and Paco had left Friday morning after the call from Credo Canyon. They drove an old pickup that Papa bought with his last money.

Papa had called on Tuesday night. "The house is ready," he said. "Come now."

The sky lightened, hiding the night stars. Only the moon showed its lopsided face.

LaReina stretched her arms and legs. "Make a wish for our new house," she said. "I wish for big windows. What about you?"

"I don't know," LeNora said. She couldn't dream about houses—houses disappeared from her dreams as quickly as they did under rivers of water. Instead she thought about Tabitha and Grandma Fransico—the givers of the quilt. She tried to give them faces. More than anything she wanted to know them.

I Wonder . . .

I wonder if you sometimes wish you could give your friend Jesus a face . . .

The Yellow House

"Credo Canyon. Here we are." Pappy's voice sounded tired but happy. LeNora sniffed her arm. It smelled like the little bars of white soap. But the smell of the stinky water stayed in her mind. She never wanted to smell like that again. One evening a well-dressed lady had given her a rose-shaped soap. It smelled like roses too. Instead of using it, she had kept it in her pocket. She took it out now and smelled it. It was the only nice thing she could give Tabitha. But it hardly seemed nice enough.

"Turn left onto Eagle View Drive." Mama read directions from a piece of paper. "Now right onto Rimrock Avenue."

"Look," called LaReina. "The yellow house. And all the people standing in the front yard. It must be our house."

"Papa," called out Huey. "I see Papa."

Pappy parked the car in the driveway. Then they all ran to hug Papa and Paco.

Papa's arms folded around the family, but LeNora wasn't in the middle of the hug. Only the tips of Papa's hands reached her. But he gave her that special wink that reminded LeNora of what Papa always told her: "You're my quiet one, my gentle one, but all the big things in your heart shout very loud."

A girl smiled at LeNora. It could be Tabitha, LeNora thought. She smiled back. Then she squeezed Papa's fingers. All the bad things about the flood didn't seem so bad.

> Even more, I consider everything to be nothing compared to knowing Christ Jesus my Lord.
>
> *Philippians 3:8a*

I Wonder . . .

I wonder if smiles from friends sometimes make your troubles seem easier . . .

Thank You

Seconds after Papa's hug, LeNora felt squished by all the people trying to say hello. She dropped to her knees and crawled out of the greeting circle.

The girl who had smiled at LeNora held out her hand. "Let me help you," she said.

LeNora felt silly for getting caught crawling between everyone's legs, but she took the outstretched hand. "Are you Tabitha?" she asked.

"I sure am. Are you LaReina or LeNora?"

"LeNora. LaReina is in the middle of the crowd. Then she's going to choose our room in the new house."

"I'm glad you're not as busy," Tabitha said. "I didn't want to wait another minute to meet you. Let's go sit on my front porch."

As LeNora followed Tabitha across the yard, all the questions she wanted to ask rushed through her mind. *Why did you send the quilt? Will we be friends?*

When they came to the porch step, Tabitha sat down. LeNora sat down beside her.

"I can't believe I'm going to live so close to you," LeNora said.

"I know," Tabitha said. "Isn't it great? We'll be like sisters."

"Thank you," LeNora said, "for the quilt, for everything."

I Wonder . . .

I wonder if there's something you want to thank your friend Jesus for . . .

To know him [Jesus Christ] is the best thing of all.

Philippians 3:8b

Roses

"When they called our names at the shelter to come to the office, I was scared," LeNora said. "I thought something else bad had happened. Then they handed us the quilt. It was so beautiful. That night I figured you were a rich princess. I couldn't understand why us, and why something so nice."

Tabitha told LeNora about the picture in the paper and Grandma's quilts.

"Come inside," Tabitha said. "We have more quilts. Grandma makes them."

LeNora followed Tabitha into the tiny house. Tabitha showed her the quilt on her bed, the one on Grandma's bed, and more in a big chest beside Grandma's bed. On the top of the chest was a glass bowl full of dried rose petals. It smelled like roses. LeNora wished she could smell like that too. Then she remembered the soap in her pocket.

"Would your Grandma like a rose soap?" she asked.

"Oh yes. Grandma loves anything with roses. You must have known that because of the rose quilt."

LeNora turned her face the other way. She hadn't thought about it before, but now it made sense.

The soap seemed to fit like part of a picture next to the glass bowl.

I Wonder . . .
I wonder if Grandma expected a gift from LeNora . . .

For me, being right with God . . . comes because I believe in Christ.

Philippians 3:9b

A Difference in Sisters

"What time is it?" LeNora asked.

"It's 5:28," Tabitha said. "The time has gone fast. There's a potluck dinner at the church at 5:30. We'd better hurry."

"LaReina," LeNora whispered. "She must be wondering what happened to me."

The girls ran outside. A large group was still by the house. LeNora looked for LaReina. Then she felt a pinch on her elbow. It was LaReina.

"I already picked the window side of the room," LaReina whispered in her ear. "You weren't around, so you have to take the closet side."

"I found Tabitha," LeNora said. "You'll like her."

"Tabitha," LaReina said. "The Tabitha from the quilt?"

"Yep, that's me," Tabitha said. "LeNora told me how the quilt found you. It worked out better than I thought it would. Now tell me how I'll be able to tell the difference between the two of you."

"LeNora is the thoughtful one," LaReina said. "She did the right thing to find you and thank you first. I'm the busy one—either talking or doing something."

Tabitha clapped her hands. "Well then, I'll be the middle one. Because I can be noisy or quiet."

I Wonder . . .

I wonder if it matters to Jesus whether we're quiet or noisy . . .

I want to know Christ better.

Philippians 3:10a

Jesus and Zacchaeus

Luke 19:1-10

Once there was a girl who didn't study and failed a math test. When the teacher handed back the papers, this girl turned her paper over so no one could see it. After school she buried it under the garbage in the trash can. She thought she was rid of it and was free from that awful grade. But her teacher called her parents in for a conference. The girl figured big trouble was coming. But to her surprise, her father didn't get angry. Instead he said, "Let's work on these math problems. I'll help you."

Jesus knows we make mistakes. And when we do, he wants us to come to him so he can make things right for us. He did it for Zacchaeus. He wants to do it for you.

Song for the Week:
"We Thank You, God," *Songs for LiFE* 38

Prayer for the Week:
Jesus, do you see me trying to cover up
the wrong things I do?
I forget that you see me.
I forget that you want me to come to you
for forgiveness.
Don't let me go into hiding, but
let me know how good it feels to be forgiven. Amen.

Paco's Way

God our Savior,
help us.

Psalm 79:9a

The step on the bunk-bed ladder creaked. Paco Ramirez stopped. He bent over to look into the bottom bunk. Was Huey still sleeping? Yes. Paco climbed down the rest of the way. He tiptoed to the closet and took out a crumpled paper bag. His heart raced with his mind. What if it wasn't there? He dumped out the contents of the bag. The heavy metal of the watchband clinked against the floor.

He pushed away the nagging voice that told him this wasn't his watch. He listened to the voice that said this watch was awesome. Josh and the other fourth-grade boys would be impressed. With this watch he was more than a boy who lost his home in a flood. He could still be popular because of what he had.

The watch dropped easily over his knuckles. The coolness of the metal settled against his arm. Quickly he pulled a gray sweatshirt over his head and covered the watch on his arm.

Huey sat up, rubbing his eyes.

"I'm leaving early for school," Paco said, "meeting Josh Henry." He smoothed down a stubborn cowlick in his black hair. "You can walk to school with the girls."

In the kitchen, Paco gulped down a glass of milk—milk that someone gave them. Again and again he was reminded of how much everyone had helped them. But he wanted to be known as a clever and cool guy—not someone who needed to be helped.

I Wonder ...
I wonder if everyone has times when they need help from someone else . . .

The Watch

As soon as Paco met with Josh, he pushed up the sleeves on his sweatshirt. He had to push up the watch on his arm too.

"Wow," Josh said. "That's a nice watch. Is it your dad's?"

Paco turned his wrist so the face of the watch caught the sunlight. "Nope, my dad's watch was ruined in the flood. Most of our good things were lost, but my watch is waterproof. Boy, was I glad I spent the extra money for this one."

"Wow," Josh said again. "It must have been expensive."

At school Josh told Peter and Trevor about Paco's watch. He told Betsy, Meghan, Alexa, and Kalle too.

"You mean you lost everything valuable except for your watch?" Alexa asked.

"That's right," Paco said.

"It's kind of big, though," Trevor said. "Doesn't it slip off your hand?"

Paco twisted the watch until it fit midway up his arm.

"Someone probably gave it to you because they felt sorry for you," Alexa said.

A red-hot pepper feeling rushed through Paco and up to his face. He made a fist. He wanted to prove something with his fists, but as the watch slid down to his knuckles, he couldn't escape the thought that this watch was stolen.

I Wonder . . .

I wonder how Paco can get out of his lie . . .

Save us and forgive our sins.

Psalm 79:9d

What Now?

Paco jammed the watch into the deepest corner of his pants pocket. For the rest of the school day, he kept his face hidden behind his new fourth-grade books.

He didn't think he imagined the strange looks Josh and the others gave him. At recess he stayed in his seat paging through his science book.

"You coming out?" Josh asked. "You can collect rocks with me or play basketball with Trevor and Peter."

"Naw," Paco said. "Science is my favorite subject. Just need to check out the book. It doesn't look as good as the one I had in my old school."

Josh didn't move away from Paco's desk. But Paco wasn't giving him another chance to offer an invitation. He shielded his eyes with his hand so Josh couldn't make eye contact. Finally Josh left to go outside.

Paco fished the watch out of his pocket, remembering when he first saw it. Half the town had bunked in the school gym that evening. All day long they had been working in waist-deep, stinking, muddy water. He saw his video games ruined by the water. His sports posters. It was all gone. But there on the counter in the men's locker room was a watch. He had picked it up—just to look at it. Then he heard footsteps and before he could think what else to do, the watch was in his pocket.

I Wonder . . .
I wonder if you know how hard it is to do the right thing after you've made a wrong choice . . .

Blessed are those whose sin the LORD never counts against them.

Psalm 32:2a

Paco's Mess

Paco remembered the large cans of chili that had been opened and heated for supper that night in the gym. Just as Paco was about to take his first spoonful, Alberto Gaspar had bellowed out in a loud voice. His watch was missing. Alberto Gaspar owned practically everything in town, including his father's business. Alberto Gaspar may have lost his house in the flood, but he had plenty of money to build again. Not like the Ramirezes, who would be left with nothing. Paco decided he deserved the watch more than a rich man. It was his father's money that let Alberto Gaspar buy such nice things in the first place.

But now the watch looked big and clumsy.

As soon as the last school bell rang, Paco ran home. The closet in his bedroom had a trap door in the ceiling. There was nothing up there—just a crawl space.

He pushed a chair under the trapdoor. He pushed it open just enough to slide the watch under a bundle of fat pink insulation.

"Paco," called Mrs. Ramirez. "Someone is here to see you."

Before Paco could get the chair out of the closet, Josh stepped into the room.

"My mom sent over a casserole," Josh said. "I—I was just wondering if you were in sort of a—you know—mess. Because if you are, I know what it's like."

Josh was poking his finger through a buttonhole on his flannel shirt, but his eyes were steady and kind. Paco believed Josh. He believed Josh wanted to care about him.

I Wonder . . .

I wonder if telling Josh about the watch would be the right thing to do . . .

> Be glad because of what the LORD has done for you.
>
> *Psalm 32:11a*

Confession and Peace

"Last fall," Josh said, "I lied to my parents so I could earn money that they didn't know about. To keep it up, I had to lie more."

"Did you think I was lying?" Paco asked.

Josh took his finger out of the buttonhole and smoothed his shirt against his belly. "Just a guess. You were sort of acting like I did."

Paco nodded. "So how did you fix your mess?"

"Told the truth," Josh said. "I was supposed to be watching Caleb after school. But I lost him and had to call my mom. Then I had to admit what I was really doing."

"Well, no one knows about the watch," Paco said. "And I'll just keep it that way."

"What about the owner?" Josh said. "He'd like it back."

Paco sat down on Huey's bunk. He sighed. Suddenly a loud bump and thud came from the closet. The ceiling square from the trap door and the watch had fallen.

"I suppose this means I should send it back to Mr. Gaspar. It sure is embarrassing though."

"I'll do it with you," Josh said. Then he patted Paco on the back. "The video store is selling dinosaur watches for $1.99 with rentals of the new dinosaur movie. We could get you one after we mail back the watch," Josh said.

"Sounds great," Paco said.

I Wonder...
I wonder why doing the right thing gives you joy . . .

Be joyful, you who do what is right!

Psalm 32:11b

Jesus and a Thankful Man

Luke 17:11-19

Have you sent any thank-you cards lately? If you haven't, think about sending one to someone just as a surprise. And be sure to tell them why you are thankful.

Sometimes it's easy to explain why we're thankful. But sometimes it's hard. If you have received a gift from a person, it is easy. You can just say thank you for the present. But what about a thank you for just being a friend or a terrific parent or grandparent? Now you have to think harder. Can you find the right words to tell someone how important he or she is to you?

The man who was cured by Jesus was thankful for the healing. He came back to say so. And then he had more reason to be thankful. He learned that faith in Jesus had healed him.

Song for the Week:
"God Is So Good," *Songs for LiFE* 207

Prayer for the Week:
Dear Jesus, you are great and
   wonderful and big.
I want to say thank you for being so good
to me. But most of all I want to say
thank you because you are Jesus,
   my Savior. Amen.

An Invitation

A trip! Marisa Riley listened to the girls in her class talk about the music festival in Silver Springs. The children's choir at Credo Canyon Church had been invited to sing in the festival. Mrs. Lenci promised them they could go if everyone learned the new songs and had permission from their parents.

It was lunchtime. Marisa planted carrot sticks in her applesauce while listening.

"This is so dreamy," Meghan said. "My cousin went with her choir last year. She had so-o-o much fun."

Alexa giggled and wiggled a dance in her seat. "My dad will drive the church bus, and guess what?! He said on the way home we could spend a couple of hours at Fantastic Waters. It's so awesome."

"Is that the place with the indoor water slides?" Betsy asked.

"That's the one," Alexa said. "It's huge. We'll have a blast."

"We have to pray that we can really go," Meghan said.

Marisa gripped the edges of the brown cafeteria tray. She loved to sing. But she had never joined the choir. And she never did much praying either. Right now if she was used to praying, she'd pray for another chance.

"Marisa," Kalle said, "would you like to join us? I'm sure Mrs. Lenci would love to have you."

I Wonder . . .
I wonder if you have ever stopped to think about someone who would like to be included in your fun . . .

Always try to be kind to each other and to everyone else.

1 Thessalonians 5:15b

The Music

Marisa's end-of-the-table seat turned into the center seat as all the girls gathered around her and made plans for teaching her the new music.

After lunch Mrs. Page always assigned silent reading. Marisa propped up her book and wondered about all that had happened so fast. Was it a prayer when she thought about praying for another chance? Maybe this prayer thing worked. Well, she'd soon find out. Learning the music would be the easy part. Talking her mother into letting her go would be the hard part.

"Please say yes, Mother," she said over and over to herself.

Meghan had an extra copy of the music at her house, so after school Marisa walked home with Meghan. The music was sitting on the piano. Both girls sat at the piano as Meghan played through one of the pieces. Marisa followed the notes and the words. The music quickly settled in her mind. But the words? A Redeemer—Jesus Christ. And thank the Father for giving the Son. The words with the music stirred something in her heart that she couldn't explain.

Slowly she walked home with the music. Singing about God and Jesus was fun for her friends. In her heart she whispered "Jesus." It sounded nice.

I Wonder . . .
I wonder if singing about Jesus will make Marisa's heart happy . . .

Always be joyful.

1 Thessalonians 5:16

Permission

Marisa hummed as she opened the apartment door.

"You're late," said her mother.

"I'm sorry," Marisa said. "I've been invited to sing with the children's choir. And three Saturdays from this one, they're going to sing at a festival in Silver Springs."

Her mother lifted a section of hair and sprayed it with short squirts from a pink bottle. "Marisa dear, you have to watch your sisters on Saturdays for the next few months."

Marisa glared at her mother's frosted blonde hair. All her mother seemed to care about was her hair and her latest boyfriend, Dennis Kirk. She didn't care about her girls. If she did, she'd figure out a way to take care of Jennifer and Renny herself.

"Mom, please. Singing with the choir is important to me."

"And working a few extra Saturdays is what's going to keep food on the table for you and your sisters."

Marisa set her face so nothing would move on it. No words from her mouth. No tears from her eyes. She hated her mom and her life. She ran to her room.

See—there wasn't a Jesus who cared. But inside her heart something said pray.

She stared at the ceiling. "Jesus, are you good? Is it just a lucky thing to pray, or is it real?"

I Wonder . . .

I wonder if Marisa's questions are kind of like a prayer . . .

I wonder if Jesus cares what words we use to pray . . .

Never stop praying.

1 Thessalonians 5:17

No Matter What

Marisa remembered she had placed the music on the counter while talking to her mom. But she didn't want to go back out there to get it. She went over the words in her head. *Redeemer.* What exactly did that mean? She searched under her bed for the dictionary.

Her finger moved down the page of r's. Redeem, redeemable, redeemer—1. One who redeems; a savior. 2. Jesus Christ, who saved people from sinfulness by his death on the cross.

It still didn't make a lot of sense. She went back up to the word redeem and read over the definitions. The seventh meaning was helpful. "To save from sin and to make up for it."

It didn't say anything about Jesus making prayers come true like wishes. But if Jesus wanted to save her from sin, then he must care. Maybe that's why there were songs about Jesus and that's why Jesus' love was such a big deal.

She thought about the times she lied to her mom. There were also times when she helped herself to money from her mother's purse. It was true her mother had to work hard to earn the money.

"Jesus, forgive me," she whispered. "Be my redeemer." It was quiet in her room, in the apartment. It was as if Jesus was listening. "Thank you," she said.

I Wonder . . .
I wonder if you know that Jesus *was* listening . . .

Give thanks no matter what happens.

1 Thessalonians 5:18a

Another Reason for Thanks

"**M**arisa," her mother called from the other side of the bedroom door. "May I come in?"

Marisa jumped up and opened the door. "Mom, I'm sorry. . . ."

"No, I'm sorry," said her mom. "You should be able to sing with the choir if that's what you want. It isn't fair for me to expect you to give up every Saturday."

They hugged each other.

"But what about work and Jennifer and Renny?" Marisa asked.

Mom chewed on the ragged edge of a broken fingernail. "There's a lady upstairs. She stopped me once after work. Said it must be hard to raise three girls by myself. And then she offered to help out anytime I got stuck."

"Is it Sophie?" Marisa asked.

"Yes, I believe that is her name."

"She'd be great," Marisa said. "Some of the other girls at school know her too. She loves to tell stories, and you know how Jennifer can listen for hours to stories."

Mom smoothed Marisa's hair. "It's time I took you to the beauty shop and got you a nice cut. Now why don't you call your friends and tell them you can go."

Marisa nodded. "In a minute. I have something else to do first."

As her mother left the room, Marisa said, "Thank you, Jesus. You are so good."

I Wonder . . .
I wonder why Marisa thanked Jesus before she called her friends . . .

God wants you to thank him because you believe in Christ Jesus.

1 Thessalonians 5:18b

Jesus and a Thankful Woman

Luke 7:36-50

Is it possible to say thank you without ever saying a word or writing a note? Last week you practiced saying thank you by sending a note. This week practice saying thank you by doing something for someone. Make a list of what others do for you; then add to that list what you could do for them.

Was God on your list? What has God done for you? You could never pay him back, but you can say thank you by what you do.

Song for the Week:
"I Will Enter His Gates," *Songs for LiFE* 9

Prayer for the Week:
All your gifts are around me, Lord.
Thank you for my home,
friends, and family.
May I show my thanks to you
and others in all that I do today. Amen.

Saying Thanks

Mrs. Ramirez set a platter of tacos on the table. Huey climbed up on his chair. He sprawled halfway across the table to reach for a crisp taco.

Mr. Ramirez caught Huey's arm before Huey's hand grabbed the taco.

"Wait for your brother and sisters," Mr. Ramirez said. "When we're all seated, we'll pray before we eat."

Huey leaned against the back of his chair and folded his arms across his chest. He was hungry. Why did they have to have this rule about praying before eating?

"Thank you for this food," Mr. Ramirez prayed. "And bless this house. We are so thankful to live here. . . ."

Huey opened one eye. All the other eyes were closed. He stretched out his hand until it touched the platter. Slowly and quietly, he pulled the platter of tacos toward him.

Then all the eyes opened. They looked at Huey who still had his hand on the platter.

"Huey!" Mr. Ramirez said. "What are you doing?"

"Praying," Huey said.

I Wonder . . .
I wonder why we close our eyes and listen during prayer . . .

Full of Thanks

"Huey doesn't know how to give thanks to God," LaReina said.

"I do so," Huey said. He pushed the taco platter back towards the center of the table. "Mama always says Jesus kept me alive when I was born. I say thank you every birthday."

Mama put the fattest taco on Huey's plate. "Yes, it was Jesus who helped my little two-pound baby live and kept him alive through all the operations."

"See." Huey stuck his tongue out at LaReina. But then he remembered his third birthday—the one in the hospital. The bed was so big and so empty without Paco beside him. He remembered trying to open his eyes for the longest time. When they finally opened, his family rushed toward him. They had balloons, stuffed animals, and wrapped-up boxes. "Happy birthday," they shouted. Then Mama whispered over and over again. "Thank you, Jesus, for keeping my boy alive." On his last birthday, just before the flood, Huey said thank you too, just because Mama said it was important.

Then the flood took away all his birthday presents, but there were new presents when they came to Credo Canyon. Yes, this was like a new birthday. And Papa said the family should say thank you every day. Thank you to God because it was God who made all these good things come to them.

I Wonder...
I wonder what's on your list of things to be thankful for...

He [God] made us, and we belong to him.

Psalm 100:3b

More than a Word

After supper Huey went to the room that he shared with Paco. He opened the top dresser drawer. And there on the top was a smooth, flat, perfectly folded, orange T-shirt. It was so new and clean he almost didn't dare put it on. But someone knew that he had lost his favorite orange T-shirt, and now this new one came with the house. There was a Monopoly game too. It had all the colored money—white, pink, green, yellow, blue, and more. He liked it better than real money. If he ever became president of the country, he'd change all the money into Monopoly money.

Papa had his way of being thankful by saying thank-you prayers. But now Huey wanted to be thankful in his own way. Everyone in Credo Canyon should get a thank-you gift. He could start with his class at school.

He pulled an empty box out of the closet. He put in his favorite new things—a Mr. Potato Head, a fake ice cube with a bug inside of it, and a word-a-day calendar.

It felt as if he smiled himself to sleep that night. In the morning he ate two extra pancakes—being thankful made him hungry. Maybe it'd even make him grow as tall as other kids his age.

At school, he sneaked inside the classroom before the bell rang. He put a gift on Lucas Barna's seat, Caleb Henry's seat, and Jennifer Jordan's seat.

"Thank you for being my new friends," he whispered when he had finished.

I Wonder . . .
I wonder if acting thankful makes you feel more thankful . . .

Give thanks to him and praise his name.

Psalm 100:4c

Giving Back

Lucas and Caleb came into the first-grade room together. Lucas went right toward the Mr. Potato Head on his seat.

"What?" said Lucas as he picked up the Mr. Potato Head. Then he mumbled something to Caleb.

Caleb went to his seat and picked up the ice cube. "He did it to me too," Caleb shouted in a loud whisper.

Lucas and Caleb quickly looked toward Huey. Then they turned away.

They don't like their gifts, Huey thought. He tugged on his orange T-shirt. It already came down to his knees, but now he wished it would swallow him up whole. He went to the reading center to hide behind the bookcase. The good thing about being so small was that it was easier to hide in small corners. And since he was new to the class, maybe even the teacher wouldn't notice that he was missing.

Lucas and Caleb came over to the reading center. They stood inches away from Huey's hiding spot.

"Isn't that Huey weird?" Lucas said.

"Yeah," Caleb said. "He gave us back the presents we gave him. But how did he know which ones came from us? Pastor Lenci just collected our stuff and put in the house so it'd look like home for Huey's family."

I Wonder...

I wonder if we can give God anything that he hasn't already given us . . .

The LORD is good.

Psalm 100:5a

Generous

Huey jumped out of his hiding spot. "I didn't know I gave you what you gave me." He lowered his head. "I just gave you what I thought you'd like—to say thank you for being my new friends."

"Well, to tell you the truth," Lucas said, "I did sort of miss my Mr. Potato Head after I gave it to you."

"Yeah," Caleb said. "And my cousins are coming next month. I've never played my ice-cube trick on them."

Huey tugged at the hem of his T-shirt. "Thanks for giving me things you liked and not just your junk. If you'd ever like to wear my T-shirt, I'll let you. It's my favorite."

Jennifer Jordan came over to the boys carrying the word-a-day calendar.

"Did you give that to me?" Huey asked.

Jennifer wrinkled her nose. "No, I thought you gave it to me."

The boys all talked at once, trying to explain what had happened.

"You guys sound like the word for today," Jennifer said, showing them the page on her word calendar. "It's *generous.* It means 'willing to give.'"

"*Generous,*" Huey said. "I like that word."

After he returned to his seat, he said a prayer. His first prayer since his birthday. He thanked God for being generous.

I Wonder . . .
I wonder if you think God is generous . . .

His faithful love
continues forever.

Psalm 100:5b

The Great Parade

Matthew 21:1-17

Do you like to sing praise songs? It can be fun to sing loud. It can be fun to sing words that you know by heart—to sing words that fit together, that rhyme, and that tell a story. Singing can even make you feel happy.

What would it have been like to shout praises to Jesus as he rode on the donkey? The palm branches that the children carried were a part of their feast days. The children waved them just like you might wave flags or balloons at a parade. The children shouted for Jesus, the King. But they only had a small idea of what kind of king Jesus would be. Do you know what kind of king he is?

Song for the Week:
"Oh, for a Thousand Tongues to Sing,"
   Songs for LiFE 19

Prayer for the Week:
Praise to you, Lord.
You are the King over all.
I shout to you.
I praise you. Amen.

Not for Paco

Paco walked five steps behind Mama, Papa, LaReina, LeNora, Huey, and Humblelina. They were going to the stone church in Credo Canyon.

At the corner of Juniper Lane, Paco gazed at the hills and rocky cliffs of Credo Canyon. That's where he wanted to be—on the nature trail next to the river that roared with water from melted snow.

Josh met him just outside the church door. His straight hair was combed to the side with a definite part along the side of his head. What was the occasion? Now Josh practically pushed him into church as if it were a big deal to be there.

"It's Palm Sunday," Josh said. "I'll get you a palm branch. All of the classes are carrying the branches and singing praise songs."

You must be kidding, Paco thought. But there in front of him were kids running, shouting, and waving green branches from palm trees.

"I have to use the bathroom," Paco said. He scooted between a group of mothers and their kids. He ran past the men's room, out the front doors, and across the parking lot to the tall junipers. The bushy spines covered him. He'd wait until church started. Then he'd run.

Shouts of "Hallelujah!" came from inside the church. Then people started singing. Paco listened. The stone church seemed to have a voice. It seemed alive.

I Wonder . . .
I wonder what things you like best about church . . .

A Small, Lonely Sound

Did Josh miss him? Did Mama, Papa, Huey, and the girls notice he was not there?

Don't give in, Paco told himself. Run before it's too late.

Without looking back, he ran. He didn't stop until he came to the signpost that marked the nature trail. Magpies squabbled in the bare branches of the scrub oak. Why did their noisy ruckus remind him of the singing in the church? It wasn't the same. It was just that they were all together making the sounds. He was the one that was not a part of it. He picked up a rock and aimed it at a tree trunk. The magpies didn't get the message, though. They gawked as loud as before.

Paco could hear the river too. It was a few feet beyond the trail. He sidestepped muddy patches that were in the shade, making his way to the river. A cluster of large boulders sat next to the river. He settled down on a boulder that had a flat lap.

Josh said the river had a name—The Thousand Tongues River. What did it mean? Was it the sound of a thousand tongues or was it thousands of tongue-like whitecaps against the rocks?

Paco clicked his tongue. It was a lonely sound. It wasn't the great sound of the singing at church, the magpies, or the river.

I Wonder . . .
I wonder how many different sounds praise God . . .

Praise our God, all you who serve him!

Revelation 19:5b

Followed

Paco picked up a few pebbles that had crumbled away from the boulder. He threw them into the river. The river swallowed them like a frog gulping down flies. Then he tried to see if his throws could reach across the river. His third pebble landed on the other side. Plop. It landed next to something that looked like a shiny, gold chain.

Paco scrambled down the boulders. Yes, his eyes weren't playing a trick on him. But how was he going to get it? He could take the trail all the way down to the bridge on Eagle View Drive and then go across. But it'd be hard to find the exact spot again.

A few feet down the river, several flat rocks rose above the water. It was enough of a bridge to take him halfway across. He could jump the last section.

Slowly he put his sneakered foot into the icy water. The rock was flat all right. Flat and smooth enough to be slippery. He talked himself through each step. Grip your toes. Take it slow. Keep a firm footing.

He made it. It took him only seconds to find the chain. It was a bright yellow gold. A cross hung on it.

"Paco, what did you find?" It was Huey.

Paco swiped up the chain and closed it up in his fist. "Did you follow me?"

"Yep."

"Well, you shouldn't have. You're supposed to be singing."

I Wonder . . .

I wonder what your favorite song is for praising God . . .

Rushing Waters

"Paco, the singing is for you too," Huey said.

"Go back," Paco yelled. He waved his arms at Huey.

"I don't know the way," Huey said. "I watched you. Not where I was going."

Paco made his way back to the stone bridge. How was he going to get Huey back to church and make him not talk about all of this? He spotted his jumping rock. He leaped. But he had forgotten about the slipperiness of the rock. In a second he was off his feet and in the water. Quickly he grabbed a tree branch that hung over the river. The cross fell out of his hand. His cigarette lighter that was his light during the darkness of the flood floated out of his shirt pocket. He saw them leave, carried away by the water.

Paco had been a fighter in the flood. And he wasn't going to give up now either. But how was he going to get out of this?

Just then the branch that he was holding onto snapped. Again he found himself in the river.

The water pushed him, pulling him away from Huey. At first he heard Huey's cries. Then all he heard was the rush of water against his head.

As fast as it started, the bumpy ride stopped. Paco opened his eyes. Water swirled calmly around him in a pool in the middle of the river. Above him the water roared over the rocks. It sounded like a huge crowd shouting—shouting with joy that he was okay.

I Wonder . . .

I wonder how many things you can think of to praise God for . . .

Then I heard the noise of a huge crowd. It sounded like the roar of rushing waters and like loud thunder. The people were shouting, "Hallelujah! Our Lord God is the King who rules over all."

Revelation 19:6

A Reason for Singing

Let us be joyful and glad! Let us give him glory!

Revelation 19:7a

"Paco, Paco. Where are you?"

"Over here," Paco called as he climbed out of the pool.

"You okay?" Huey asked.

"Just took a little ride down the river," Paco said. Could he tell Huey how scared he was? Then how alive he felt? It was as if he had been given another chance to live.

The water sloshed and squished inside his sneakers with each step that he took. "Let's go home."

"You never told me what you found," Huey said.

"It was a cross," Paco said. "A gold one. But I lost it in the river."

"Wow," Huey said. "There's a cross at the church. I'll show it to you."

Paco wrung water out of his shirt. Churches, crosses, singing, and the roaring river. He had never had a Sunday morning like this one.

"Let's run," he said, grabbing Huey's hand. "I'll change my clothes. Then we might get to church before it's over."

The people in the church were quietly listening when the boys returned. Paco went inside. Huey followed him. They found an empty seat in the back.

Then everyone stood to sing. Paco listened to the words. The singing had a joyful sound, just like the river. Was it the joy of being alive, or was there something more?

I Wonder . . .
I wonder if you have a reason to sing praises to the Lord today . . .

The Footwashing
John 13:1-17

Babies and toddlers like their feet. Others like the feet of babies too. But a few years later, those same feet are more stinky than sweet. Now those feet aren't so easy to like. It takes a lot of love to want to take care of not-so-sweet feet.

Jesus washed his disciples' feet. He did it to show his love for them. Today washing feet is not part of the way you treat a guest. But loving them enough in other servantlike ways is still a test of great love. Can you think of a servantlike way to love others?

Song for the Week:
"Jesus, Jesu, Fill Us with Your Love," *Songs for LiFE* 251

Prayer for the Week:
Jesus, I need a greater kind of love
than the one I have for my friends.
I need the kind of love that is strong enough
to love when it isn't easy.
Thank you for your
   big love for me. Amen.

Uh-umm

Meghan squeezed the juice of a lemon into a cup of warm water. She added a teaspoon of honey. With one gulp, she drank all of it.

"Uh-umm." She forced sounds out of her throat on the way to the piano. Her fingers played the notes just right, but her voice didn't match the notes.

"Meghan, dear," her mother said, "you have a bad case of laryngitis. I'll call Mrs. Lenci and tell her you won't be able to sing the solo."

"Mom," Meghan shouted with a hoarse whisper. "Singing a solo for the choir trip is the best thing that has ever happened to me. And it'll be the worst thing if I don't get to sing."

Mrs. Bennett put her arm around her daughter. "I'm sorry."

"Marisa Riley," Meghan said just above a whisper, "thinks my solo is the best part of our program."

"I'm proud of you for inviting Marisa to join the choir," Mrs. Bennett said. "I could tell she liked your solo. She listened to you every day. In fact, I bet she knows it as well as you do. You know, Meghan, Marisa could sing it."

Meghan gulped through her tight throat. Marisa had a sweet voice. But this was her part, not Marisa's. It'd be better to have a hole in the program than to let Marisa take her part.

I Wonder . . .
I wonder if you ever find it hard to let someone take your place . . .

> All of you, put on a spirit that is free of pride toward each other as if it were your clothes.
>
> *1 Peter 5:5*

Meghan's Choice

Meghan took her music off the piano. It was true Marisa did know this music too. But turning over the music to Marisa was like turning over her dreams. What if Marisa took the part and did a better job? No, that wasn't possible. Was it?

Mrs. Bennett interrupted Meghan's thoughts. "Do you want me to call Mrs. Lenci? I could tell her your problem and ask about Marisa taking your place."

Meghan twisted the gold musical-note earring in her right ear. "I—I think Marisa might be scared. Have you noticed how she'll cover her mouth?"

"You may be right," Mrs. Bennett said? "You know her better than I do. Why don't you talk to Marisa first? See if you can find out how she feels about it."

Meghan nodded. Silently, she put on her coat and headed outside. She'd walk around the block and then come home to tell her mom that Marisa wasn't interested.

Next to the driveway purple crocus petals fanned out toward the sun. Slivers of yellow showed through the green buds of the daffodils. A few tulips were almost ready to open. Meghan bent over to smell the buds. This was her favorite time of the year. Every flower had its chance to show off its colors.

She sat beside the flower bed. Maybe Marisa needed a chance too. A chance to use her voice for everyone to hear. Meghan plucked a bright, showy crocus.

I Wonder . . .
I wonder if Meghan is going to make the right choice . . .

So don't be proud. Put yourselves under God's mighty hand.

1 Peter 5:6a

Too Hard To Let Go

"**M**eghan."

Marisa was coming down Stepping Stone Avenue. She wore her old tan pants that were an inch above her socks. If she did sing, what would she wear? Nothing in her wardrobe was really nice.

Meghan pretended to be busy with the flowers. But it was hard to avoid Marisa when she sat down on the driveway.

"Are you excited about tomorrow?" Marisa asked.

Meghan cupped her hand over her throat. "I have laryngitis," she whispered. "I can't sing."

Marisa groaned. "In my dreams last night, I saw you singing. You were wearing your black jumper with the pink sweater. Your long black curls touched your cheeks and your shoulders. And you sounded as beautiful as you looked."

That dream matched Meghan's.

"There are all kinds of things I can do to get my voice back," Meghan said. "I'm going to wrap warm towels around my neck. And drink tea with lemon juice and honey."

"I'll pray for you," Marisa said. "Prayer works, don't you think?"

Meghan nodded. She forced a smile too. But her heart didn't feel right. If Marisa talked to God about this, God would know the real story.

I Wonder . . .
I wonder if it is hard for you to talk to God when you don't feel loving towards someone else . . .

A New Dream

"I think you should go inside and rest now," Marisa said. "I'll go to the store and get you throat lozenges. There's a kind that might help."

Meghan watched Marisa walk down Juniper Street toward the shops on Rimrock Avenue. Then she quietly slipped inside of her house. She went to her room and wrapped herself in her puffy quilt. But it was no use to rest. Monsters seemed to fill up her room. And she was the biggest monster—the meanest too.

The only thing that made the monsters leave was remembering the sound of Marisa's voice. Her sweet, musical voice. And her caring words. Funny, she never thought of Marisa being so kind. But she had changed since she had joined the choir. Maybe the words of the songs changed Marisa.

She could almost hear Marisa sing the solo. Her voice was clear and gentle.

Meghan tossed off her quilt. Somewhere in her closet she had a pale, green pantsuit. It never looked exactly right on her. But it'd be perfect for Marisa.

There was a soft knock on her door. It was Marisa.

"Your brother let me in the house," Marisa said. "I found the drops."

"I won't need them," Meghan said. "I have a better idea. You can sing the solo."

"Me?"

"Yes," Meghan said, showing Marisa the pantsuit. "I had a dream . . ."

I Wonder . . .
I wonder what changed Meghan's feelings about Marisa . . .

So you will only have to suffer for a little while.

1 Peter 5:10b

For Keeps

The next morning, Meghan woke up to the birds chirping outside her window. It was only 5:00—too early. She needed her rest. Mom said she could go along with the choir if she felt okay. It wasn't that she really felt sick yesterday; it was just her voice.

Her voice. Was it better or worse? "Good morning," she sang out loud.

It worked. She tried a scale. No problem. All that worry yesterday for nothing.

But how would she tell Marisa? It was like magic to see Marisa's face when she practiced the solo with Mrs. Lenci.

Alexa and Kalle had been surprised when they heard about Marisa taking the solo. But then they had joined in the fun—dressing up Marisa and trying new styles in her hair. The best part was her voice, though. It fit the song perfectly. Meghan was happy for Marisa. Her ugly feeling about Marisa was gone.

But now thoughts against Marisa were coming back.

She put her head on the windowsill. A fat robin came close to her. It didn't sing; it just sat there. "What should I do?" she whispered to the robin.

Three hours later, when the choir members met at the church, all the girls gathered around Marisa to tell her how excited they were for her.

Then they asked Meghan how she was feeling. Meghan smiled. She just pointed to her throat. Then she wrapped her arm around Marisa's waist as they boarded the bus.

I Wonder . . .

I wonder if God can make you strong enough to show love to others—even when it's *really* hard . . .

Then God himself will build you up again. He will make you strong and steady.

1 Peter 5:10c

A Sad Night

Matthew 26:31-46, 69-75

If you travel through a mountain pass, you may see signs that tell you to watch out for falling rocks or deer crossings. Rocks or deer can take you by surprise. If you are not prepared, an accident could happen.

Jesus warned his disciples to watch too. He told them to watch and pray. They didn't know what was going to happen to Jesus. He wanted them prepared. But they didn't prepare themselves. Peter was so unprepared that he did exactly what he said he would never do.

What about you? Are you always prepared? Or do you find yourself in situations that cause you to disappoint Jesus, others, and yourself?

Be on the alert. Watch. Pray. Always remember that Jesus loves you.

Song for the Week:
"Oh, How He Loves You and Me," *Songs for LiFE* 163

Prayer for the Week:
Jesus, I know about your love.
I know how you want me to act.
But sometimes I'm not careful.
I'm not watching out.
I don't know what is going
    to happen today.
But make me ready to act,
    knowing your great love
is right beside me. Amen.

Borrowed and Lost

Ellie watched Betsy take string, cards, and photographs out of her top dresser drawer.

"I've looked everywhere," Betsy said. "I still can't find my cross necklace."

"You could buy a new one," Ellie said.

"It wouldn't be the same. Mom and Dad Barna gave me this one the first Easter I knew about Jesus."

Ellie sat on her hands at the edge of her bed. If only she could give the necklace back to Betsy. A few weeks ago she had just felt like wearing Betsy's necklace. There didn't seem to be any harm in wearing it to school for one day. After all, she used to take whatever she wanted whenever. She had never felt guilty about it. But this time it was different. And now the necklace couldn't be returned because it was lost.

Ellie saw a wet line run down Betsy's cheek.

If it'd make Betsy feel better, she'd give up all of the gold chains that hung over her dresser doorknobs. But it wasn't gold that Betsy wanted. It was the cross.

"I'll spend the rest of my life looking for your necklace," Ellie said. If only she knew where it had slipped off and disappeared. She hadn't wanted to hurt Betsy—Betsy, the first one who really loved her.

I Wonder . . .
I wonder why Betsy's love made Ellie feel so bad . . .

"Watch and pray. Then you won't fall into sin when you are tempted."

Matthew 26:41a

Ellie's Plan

"Ellie Coman!" Betsy said, rolling her chair over to Ellie. "You say the wildest things. You don't need to search for my necklace your whole life! The cross is a nice reminder for me—that's all."

"You wouldn't love me forever if I found it?"

"I love you forever already," Betsy said. "Come on. Let's go to Alexa's house. She invited us to paint Easter eggs."

Betsy strapped the armbands of her leg crutches around her upper arms and wrists.

"Take your wheelchair today," Ellie said. From now on she'd do everything for Betsy. Never again would she disappoint her. Soon it wouldn't make any difference that she had lost the cross.

"I need the exercise," Betsy said.

Ellie followed Betsy's back-and-forth, uneven steps to Alexa's house.

At Alexa's house there was a big bowl of white eggs on the table. Smaller bowls were filled with inky dark reds, purples, blues, and yellows. There were also trays with crayons, sequins, and bits and pieces of fabrics.

I Wonder . . .
I wonder what's the best way for Ellie to show she is really sorry . . .

> "The spirit is willing. But the body is weak."
>
> *Matthew 26:41b*

A Close Call

Betsy drew with a white crayon on the white egg. Ellie watched. What was Betsy trying to do? Then she dipped the egg into the bowl of inky purple liquid. Out came a purple egg with a white cross in the center.

All the girls exclaimed how beautiful it was. Ellie didn't say anything. This whole thing about crosses was becoming a bit annoying. Wasn't Easter about flowers and bunnies? Crosses just didn't seem as much fun.

The buzzer rang on the stove. Alexa got up to rinse cold water over another batch of eggs. "I've invited Paco and Josh to join us," she said. "Paco told me he loves to paint Easter eggs. Can you believe that?"

Kalle laughed. "I know. Paco acts tough on the playground, but during art class he tries harder than anyone else."

"I think he has a tattoo," Meghan said.

"Shh," Alexa said. "I think the boys are here." She got up to let Paco and Josh in through the kitchen door.

"Look at Betsy's egg," Kalle said as the boys came over to the table.

"Nice cross," Paco said. "That reminds me. I saw a gold cross on a chain. It was beside the river along the trail. I had it in my hand, but then I lost it again."

Ellie took in a deep breath and held it while watching Betsy.

I Wonder . . .
I wonder what Ellie is thinking . . .

Another Cross

Betsy was quiet. She didn't ask what the cross looked like. She didn't say that she had lost a cross necklace and that this one might be hers. Betsy seemed too quiet.

Ellie reached for the dish of red dye. Thinking more about Betsy than the dish, Ellie set the dye at the edge of the table. In a second it was off the table and on her lap.

A fast-spreading blotch of red stained Ellie's white sweatshirt and pants.

The boys laughed, and Ellie wondered if her face was as red as her clothes. Alexa dabbed the red wetness with a wad of paper towels.

"Why don't you change into some of my clothes," Alexa said. "Then I can soak your things in the wash basin."

In the bathroom upstairs Ellie changed into a pair of jeans and a T-shirt. But she didn't want to face the others again, so she quietly took one step at a time and then slipped out the front door. She walked past her house and toward the nature trail. Maybe she could find the necklace where Paco had dropped it.

"Ellie," called a voice as she walked past the Ingels' house. It was Mrs. Ingel. "I was just about to bring a treat over to your house." Mrs. Ingel pulled back a checkered napkin from the pan. "They're hot-cross buns," she said.

Ellie stared at the rows of round-topped buns. Each one had a neat, white cross made out of frosting.

I Wonder . . .
I wonder if it would help Ellie to know that a cross stands for God's love to all those who have done wrong things . . .

Give me back the joy that comes from being saved by you.

Psalm 51:12a

Royal Treatment

"I make these rolls every year at Easter time," Mrs. Ingel said. "The crosses remind me that even though none of us are good enough to belong in God's family, he welcomes us with loving, open arms."

Ellie studied the fat, frosting crosses. "What if someone keeps on lying? And what if they never learn to tell the truth?"

Mrs. Ingel put her arm around Ellie. "Let's go back to my house. We'll have a hot-cross bun and a glass of juice."

Ellie followed Mrs. Ingel, wondering if it'd be a good idea to tell Mrs. Ingel the whole story or if it'd be better to just run away right now.

Once they were inside of the house, Ellie decided she was trapped. But Mrs. Ingel didn't start with questions. Instead she put pretty little dishes on the table and lighted a candle. She pulled out the chair for Ellie as if Ellie were a very important guest.

The bun smelled sweet and spicy. Ellie knew she wanted to eat it.

Mrs. Ingel opened her hand toward Ellie. Slowly Ellie put her hand inside the white, wrinkled hand.

"Dear Jesus, help this precious girl to know your love."

Ellie peeked at the cross on her bun. Yes, she'd fix things with Betsy.

I Wonder...
I wonder if there are times when you think it must be hard for God to love you...

Give me a spirit that obeys you. That will keep me going.

Psalm 51: 12b

Jesus Died / Jesus Lives!

Matthew 27:27-66; 28:1-10

If you lied to your friend and she found out, it could end your friendship.

Lies and other sins separate us from God too. But God loved us so much that he wanted to fix things between us. So he sent Jesus to die for our sins.

When Jesus died, the disciples were left alone; they were frightened and sad. And for the first time ever, Jesus had to leave God completely and die on the cross. It was such a terrible day that the earth shook, and darkness covered the earth in the middle of the day.

But three days later it all turned around. Jesus returned to life. He got rid of the terrible result of our sins. He brought God and people together.

Now the disciples knew the real power of their Master. And we can know that nothing can separate us from Jesus. He has the power to forgive us—and to help our friends forgive us too.

Song for the Week:
"He Is Lord," *Songs for LiFE* 178

Prayer for the Week:
Thank you, Jesus, for taking my sins.
Now I can talk to you.
I can have you as a friend.
And I can jump with joy,
knowing I have love, peace, and life in my heart.
    Amen.

Good Friday

Betsy remembered last year when she was getting ready for Good Friday night at church. She remembered how special it felt to put on the cross necklace.

Ellie came up behind Betsy. "I have a surprise for you. It's a new necklace."

A tiny cross hung from a thin chain in Ellie's hand.

"It's pretty," Betsy said. "But it isn't your fault that I lost my cross."

"Yes it is," Ellie said half whispering. "I took your necklace and lost it. I'm really sorry. I thought a new one would help you forgive me."

The necklace trembled in Ellie's thin hand.

Betsy felt sick to her stomach. Ellie was wrong—a new necklace couldn't make up for being sneaky. If Ellie had told the truth in the first place, it would have been better.

Outside the window, the setting sun barely made its way through the clouds above Credo Canyon.

Betsy lifted herself out of the wheelchair, strapped on her crutches, and hobbled past Ellie. She walked to the garage, climbed into the van, and waited for the others. Her head throbbed. Did she do the right thing, walking out on Ellie?

She checked her watch. What was taking the rest of the family so long? They were never this late. Finally the crew came with Mrs. Barna at the tail end. Betsy could see a worried look on Mom Barna's face. Did she know about the necklace?

I Wonder . . .
I wonder what made Betsy the most upset . . .

He [Jesus] obeyed God completely, even though it led to his death. In fact, he died on a cross.

Philippians 2:8b

Stolen Money?

Mom Barna buckled Molly into the seat next to Betsy.

"What's wrong?" Betsy asked.

Mom's tired face looked sad. "I misplaced my offering money, that's all," Mom said. "I'm sure it'll turn up somewhere."

Mom always put the offering money in the vase that sat on the fireplace mantel. There was never any mistake about it. The tiny golden cross flashed in Betsy's mind. Did Ellie take the offering money to buy the cross? The more Betsy thought about it, the more suspicious she became.

Ellie climbed to the very back of the van. And as they rode to church, Betsy wished she knew what was inside Ellie's head.

When they got to church, the lights were low. The darkness added to Betsy's heavy heart. She sat in the semi-darkness, wondering when they were going to put on more lights and get started.

But the lights stayed low. Soon Pastor Lenci invited the people to come up to the front and kneel on the wide step. He gave a cube of bread and a thimble of red juice to Mrs. Barna, who was kneeling beside Betsy. Then he placed his hand on Betsy's head. "May God's love and forgiveness fill you with peace," he said.

He said words like that to Ellie too. Ellie sniffed.

I Wonder . . .

I wonder if your heart has ever felt mixed-up like Betsy's . . .

> When the name of Jesus is spoken, everyone's knee will bow to worship him.
>
> *Philippians 2:10a*

A Story

As if it wasn't dark enough, Pastor Lenci blew out a candle. Then another. After each candle was blown out, there was silence. Finally Pastor Lenci picked up the Christ candle and placed it behind a table.

The darkness swallowed the whole room. Darkness, Jesus dying on a cross, Ellie's sneakiness, her anger at Ellie—it all pinched Betsy's heart.

They left the church in silence. Streams of dark rain acted like prison bars, locking in Betsy's heavy feelings.

At home, Dad Barna started a fire in the fireplace and read a story about a stranger who came to a town with gifts for everyone. Soon people in the town changed. No longer were they selfish or mean. They became like the stranger, giving gifts.

Betsy gave Dad a big hug after that story. She wished that stranger would visit the Barna house. After cups of hot cocoa, it was time for bed. Betsy and Ellie hadn't said a word to each other. That didn't change as they got ready for bed.

During the night, Betsy heard whimpering noises coming from Ellie's bed. At first Betsy just listened. The noises didn't get louder, but they didn't stop either. Betsy pulled the covers over her head. But the covers didn't shut out Ellie's muffled crying.

"What should I do?" Betsy prayed. Then she crawled out of her bed and kneeled beside Ellie.

I Wonder . . .
I wonder how Jesus is like the stranger in Dad Barna's story . . .

Everyone's mouth will say that Jesus Christ is Lord.

Philippians 2:11a

Saturday's Gift

"**I**'m here," Betsy touched Ellie's cheek. It was hot and wet. She pushed back Ellie's damp bangs. A small gift. Was that what Dad's story whispered in her heart?

In the silence and darkness of the night, Betsy rubbed Ellie's back until Ellie finally fell asleep.

Then Betsy climbed back into her own bed. She stared at the ceiling. Jesus gave her gifts every day—the gift of a family that loved her, the gift of operations that helped her walk, the gift of forgiveness. Jesus was like the stranger in the story. She wanted to be like Jesus. Then she fell asleep.

When Mom Barna knocked on the door announcing breakfast, Betsy realized she hadn't thought of what to do for Ellie.

Ellie climbed out of bed and sat on Betsy's bed. Her eyes were swollen. "Thanks for rubbing my back last night. I dreamed you were the stranger who gave me a gift."

Betsy squeezed Ellie's hand and wondered what else she could do for Ellie.

The cross on a chain was laying in a small heap on the corner of the dresser. Ellie picked it up. "I'll show this to Mom Barna and tell her the whole story."

Together the girls told Mom Barna what had happened. Then Ellie returned the necklace to the store and put the offering money back in its special place until Easter morning.

I Wonder . . .
I wonder if anyone in your life has given you the gift of forgiveness . . .

Are you cheerful because you belong to Christ? Then make my joy complete by agreeing with each other.

Philippians 2:1a, 2a

The Gift of Easter

Does his love
comfort you?
Have the same
love.

Philippians 2:1b, 2b

"Rise and shine." Ellie tapped Betsy on the shoulder.

Betsy ducked further under her covers. It was still dark. Then she remembered it was Easter morning. And they were going to meet everyone from church up on the rocks of Credo Canyon. From there they were going to sing and watch the sunrise.

Ellie was singing already. "I feel like I'm rushing out to meet Jesus," she said.

It felt that way to Betsy too, so she hurried to get dressed in the warm clothes she had set out the night before.

Dad Barna had rigged up a special seat for Betsy so they could carry her over the rough path and up the hills of Credo Canyon.

As they came near a nook surrounded by rocks, they heard voices singing.

"This is the day that the Lord has made! Rejoice! Rejoice, and be exceeding glad!"

As everyone sang "Hal-le-lu-jah," glowing sunlight filled the sky and the canyon.

Just before Dad Barna was ready to hoist Betsy up to the others, a reflection in the river caught Betsy's eye. "Stop," she said, pointing to a small pool in the river.

Dad put Betsy down. Then she reached into the pool and lifted out a shiny cross. Her lost cross. She held it tightly for a second. Then she turned to Dad. "This is the gift I've been looking for—a gift for Ellie."

I Wonder . . .
I wonder why Betsy wants to give the cross to Ellie . . .

On the Road to Emmaus
Luke 24:13-49

Imagine that you are on the school playground. Your best friend runs off to play with someone else. So you go to the swings by yourself, feeling sad. Suddenly a person jumps onto the swing next to you. It's your best friend! Together you swing higher and higher, laughing and sharing secrets. You are happy that your friend is with you again.

The two friends who were walking to Emmaus thought that the man who walked with them was just a stranger. How surprised they were when the stranger taught them all the things they wanted to know about Jesus. When they came to Emmaus, suddenly they realized that he *was* Jesus! They were talking to the person who they thought was gone from their lives forever. How happy they were to be with Jesus again!

But best of all they realized Jesus was more than an ordinary friend. He had the power to give life and be with them forever.

Song for the Week:
"Day by Day," *Songs for LiFE* 221

Prayer for the Week:
Give me the right kind of eyes to see you.
Give me the right kind of heart to know
you are always there.
Give me the right kind of thoughts
to understand all you have done for me.
Thank you for your greatness. Amen.

Too Many Comments

Huey wanted to cover his ears. The Ramirez house was filled with aunts, uncles, and big cousins. All they did was eat Mama's food and talk about Mama's kids. They didn't even notice that Mama's kid Huey was sitting by the kitchen table finishing the last piece of pie. They talked about him right while he sat there.

"Will Huey's head always be lopsided?" Aunt Dolorita whispered loudly.

"Huey will always be small," Aunt Rufina said. "It's too bad he was born early."

"He's doing just fine," Mama said. "The doctors and hospitals were wonderful. Not every child survives being born early and then having a brain tumor."

"I'd worry about him keeping up with the other kids," Aunt Dolorita said.

"Or having another tumor and costing your family all your savings," Aunt Rufina said. "Perhaps you should move back to Mexico."

"We're just fine," Mama said. "And we like living in Credo Canyon. Our new friends are like family."

"Huey could have another brain tumor, or there could be a flood like in Texas," Aunt Dolorita said. "Then what would you do?"

Huey had heard enough. But were the aunts right? Was it his fault that the family had to move and then use up all their money to pay hospital bills instead of buying flood insurance? His family would be better off if they didn't have to take care of him.

I Wonder...
I wonder if the things that go wrong ever seem stronger than the good things in your life . . .

A Runaway

Huey walked right past his aunts and out the door.

He ran as fast as his short legs could move until he reached the nature trail. A rabbit darted past him. He ran with the rabbit, creeping under and through bushes. He felt like nothing could stop him—until he tripped over a fat, gnarly root.

Huey's hands stung. Little beads of blood bubbled out of the dirt covering the heels of his hands. He sat down on a large, white boulder. It helped to press his hands together.

The sun's rays fell right on top of his head. Running away without food or water wasn't a good idea. All he had in his pockets was a wrapped, chewed piece of bubble gum. Besides, most runaways he heard about told their parents they were running away. Yes, he'd go home and take care of all that. If the family didn't have to worry about caring for him anymore, they might give him what he needed to live in the woods.

But which way was home? He stood up and turned in every direction. If only he had followed a path.

The rock on which he stood was on the top edge of a valley. Far below, he saw a path. Carefully he eased himself down from one boulder and onto another one. The path was further away than he had thought. He moved faster, going from one boulder to another.

But he was still above the path. He wiped his sweaty forehead. Several pebbles sprinkled down from above him. Was someone up there? Someone who could help him?

I Wonder . . .

I wonder if God ever turns away from a person who needs more help than others . . .

> You will know that the things God's people will receive are rich and glorious.
>
> *Ephesians 1:18b*

The Whistle

Huey listened. There were no more pebbles. But then he heard a whistle. It wasn't a bird. Only a person could whistle like that.

Perhaps the person was on the path. But where was the path? Huey noticed that the tree beside him was black. Most of the branches were stripped off of it. Probably fire. But how did it start on fire? Then he remembered a program on TV about a forest fire. It was started by lightening. He looked up in the sky. There were a couple of dark clouds. What if a storm with lightening came?

Huey stepped sideways to the next rock. It was a big, wide rock. But it wobbled underneath him. Quickly he jumped to the ground below. Sharp prickles jabbed through his already tender hands. He had landed on a cactus.

With tears in his eyes, Huey tried to pull out the tiny cactus needles. More than anything he wanted to run into his mama's arms. Mama always held him. She always told him not to worry because she would always be there for him.

Maybe being born two months early, having operations, and growing little by little wasn't as bad as being alone.

Over the chirping of the birds and the wind in the trees, Huey heard the whistling again. Paco could whistle. Maybe it was Paco. And Paco could take him back to Mama.

I Wonder . . .
I wonder what difference it makes to you to know God is with you at all times—even when you feel lost . . .

And you will know his great power. It can't be compared with anything else.

Ephesians 1:19a

The Whistle at Work

The whistling came closer. Huey listened. It sounded familiar. He had sung that song before. It could have been this morning at sunrise.

He closed his stinging eyes, remembering all the people who stood by Thousand Tongues River. The singing made all the different people blend into one, and he had been part of them.

The closer the whistling came, the more familiar it sounded.

"This is the day," he sang. Yes, that was it. But what came next? What was the part that made him so happy?

Then the whistling came so close, it was right next to him. He looked up. It was Paco!

"You got too friendly with that cactus," Paco said.

Huey swiped the dust and tears off his face with the top of his hand. Then he held out his stickered hand to Paco.

Paco opened his Swiss Army knife and pulled out a tweezers. He worked on the bristly little prickles. "This time *I* followed you," he said.

"Thanks," Huey said. "Whistling the song was a good idea. It made me braver."

"I wish I could remember all the words to the song," Paco said. "But I know it's about Jesus being alive."

I Wonder . . .
I wonder what difference it makes that Jesus is alive . . .

It [God's great power] is at work for us who believe.

Ephesians 1:19b

Back Home

It is like the
mighty strength
God showed
when he raised
Christ from the
dead.

Ephesians 1:19c-20a

"**A**re you ready to go home?" Paco asked.

Huey scratched an itchy spot on his leg. "I want to say goodbye to Mama, Papa, the girls, and Pappy. But then I have to run away again."

"That's too bad," Paco said. "It'll be hard to survive without you."

"What do you mean?" Huey asked.

Paco dug a pack of gum out of his pocket. "Well, who will help me chew a new pack of gum? Who will be my brother? And who will Mama give that extra bit that is always left over from her big dinners?"

Mama always saved the extras for Huey. Just in case he got hungry between meals. And lately that happened every day.

"But I've caused the family a lot of trouble," Huey said. "All the money to keep me alive in the beginning and all the money for the operations."

"Yeah," Paco said. "You've been a bit of trouble. But then so have I. And just think about LaReina and LeNora—nothing is more work than twins. As for Humblelina, well, she's a singer and a dancer, so she'll need all kinds of attention."

Huey took the piece of gum that Paco offered. "Let's go home," he said.

I Wonder . . .

I wonder if you can be braver when you know that your family is there for you . . .

Thomas, the Doubter

John 20:24-31

Once there was a two-year-old girl who always touched her food with her pointer finger before she'd pick it up to eat it. She had to check if it was hot. If it passed that test, she checked the texture. Anything too slippery she ignored. Her touch told her what she wanted.

What about you? What sense do you trust? Most likely it is more than one, but what if you had to believe something was real without using any of your senses? Could you do it?

The disciple Thomas thought he had to touch and see Jesus before he could believe that Jesus was alive. Then Jesus taught Thomas that there was another way: faith—believing in what Jesus said would happen.

We have to have faith, too, when it comes to Jesus. We have to trust what he taught his disciples about faith and believing in God.

Song for the Week:
"Believe in the Lord," *Songs for LiFE* 223

Prayer for the Week:
Jesus, I can't touch your hand.
I can't see your face.
I can't smell your skin.
I can't hear your voice.
But you can touch my heart.
You can fill my mind.
And you can bring joy to my soul.
I believe in you. Amen.

The New Super Store

"Grand opening for Maxmillins today," Mr. Bennett said at Saturday's breakfast.

"Awesome," Timothy said. "Can we go?"

"Yes, let's go," Meghan said. "I've heard it's a super store to beat all stores."

"We do need groceries," Mrs. Bennett said. "And new towels, and . . ."

Mr. Bennett laughed. "I'm almost sorry I mentioned it. But they also sell tires. And the tread is getting bare on the jeep's tires."

When the Bennetts got to Maxmillins, they decided Meghan would go with Mom and Timothy would go with Dad. And then they'd all meet at the food arena at noon.

Dad and Timothy passed a big cardboard display of baseball shoes. Timothy touched the smooth leather and the spikes.

"Can I look at these while you look at tires?" Timothy asked.

Dad paused. "Well, okay. See the clock up there? Meet me right here at 10:15. And don't leave the shoe department."

Timothy found a pair that he thought would fit him. He tried them on. Nope. They were bigger than they looked. He tried three more pairs. No good. He looked for a salesperson. After the woman measured his foot, he tried on a pair that was perfect.

"Do you want these?" she asked.

Timothy looked up at the clock. 10:30. Where was Dad? Did he forget to come?

I Wonder . . .
I wonder if Timothy should be afraid because he doesn't see his dad . . .

God didn't give us a spirit that makes us weak and fearful.

2 Timothy 1:7a

Missing

"I have to find my dad," Timothy said to the salesperson. "I'll be back. Don't put my shoes away."

He went back to the display. No Dad. He walked around the entire shoe department. Still no Dad. He checked the clock again. Had he read the clock correctly? He always had the correct times on clocks on his math papers. Yes, it had to be right. The big hand was moving past 10:30.

Dad must have meant meet him at the tire department at 10:15. Yes, that had to be it. Quickly Timothy ran in the direction that Dad had taken.

He hurried past camping stoves and fishing poles. It'd be nice to check out a new pole, but he didn't stop. He passed an aisle of baseballs and gloves too. But where were the tires?

A man in a blue shirt that said "Maxmillins" above the pocket was organizing a shelf of batteries.

"Where are the tires?" Timothy asked.

"Go to the far wall," the man said, "and then turn left."

The man motioned with his hand. Timothy took off in that direction. Left, left, he told himself. Then he smelled the rubbery odor of tires. He ran past rows of big, fat, black tires. But no Dad. "Dad," he cried softly, "are you looking for me too?"

I Wonder . . .

I wonder if you know how Timothy is feeling . . .

He [God] gave us a spirit that gives us power and love.

2 Timothy 1:76

Back Again

But I'm not ashamed. I know the One I have believed in.

2 Timothy 1:12b

Another Maxmillin man was taking a fat tire off the rack. Timothy went up to him.

"Have you seen my dad?" Timothy asked. "He was looking at tires."

The man let the tire bounce on the floor. "Do you know what kind of tires?"

Timothy shook his head.

"What does your dad look like?" asked the man.

Timothy thought. His dad was a tall man with dark hair, but so was the tire man. His nose and ears were just that. How could he describe his dad? Then he thought about Dad's hands. He could see Dad's long smooth fingers handling papers at the print shop. He could see Dad placing his hand over Timothy's own hand when teaching Timothy how to hold the fishing pole or the baseball bat.

"He has long fingers," Timothy said. "And there are short, black hairs on his fingers just above the knuckles. Oh, yes, and he wears a special gold ring that looks like three strands woven together. My mom gave it to him—she loves him too."

The Maxmillin man smiled. "Your dad must be a special man. But are you sure you're supposed to meet him here?"

Timothy shook his head. No, he wasn't sure. But he was sure that his dad wasn't the kind to trick him and not meet him.

I Wonder . . .

I wonder if you can tell how Timothy feels about his dad . . .

Promises

Then Timothy remembered what else his dad had said. "Don't leave the shoe department."

He had nodded his agreement to Dad, so Dad would keep that as a promise.

"I have to go now," he said to the Maxmillin tire man. "If you see my dad, tell him I'm at the shoes, just like I said I would be."

Then he ran. This time he didn't even notice the camping gear or the baseballs.

When he reached the baseball shoe display, he stopped to slow down his breathing. A boy and his mother were standing next to the display.

"But I need these shoes," the boy said. "You don't care about what is important to me."

"It's the money," the mother said. "They cost more than I have."

The boy threw the shoes on the floor and walked away. The mother picked out three pairs of shoes for herself and seemed to forget about her boy.

Timothy knew that scene wouldn't happen with his dad. He'd get an honest answer from his dad. He picked up the shoes that the boy had tossed. He wished that the boy had a dad like his. But where was his dad? If only they could hold hands in the store just like they did when he was younger.

I Wonder . . .

I wonder how you like to be treated by people in your family . . .

My son, be strong in the grace that is found in Christ Jesus.

2 Timothy 2:1

Reunion

As Timothy put the shoes back on the display, a hand reached over to help him.

"Dad! Boy, am I glad to see you." He slipped his hand into Dad's. "Have you been here the whole time?" Timothy asked.

Dad shifted a shopping bag to his other hand. "Since 10:15. First I waited around the display. Then I walked through the entire shoe department five times."

"I'm sorry," Timothy said. "At 10:15 I was trying on shoes. I forgot about the time. And then when I came to the display you were gone."

"Hmm," Dad said. "We must have been going in circles around these tall shelves, just missing each other. I never left the shoe department. The salesperson saw you, though, so I knew you were somewhere around here."

Timothy stared at the floor. He was glad Dad didn't wander away—it would have taken another hour or more to find each other then.

"Here." Dad handed Timothy the shopping bag. "The salesperson told me this was the pair that fit you."

"Dad, I can't take these. The reason you couldn't find me is because I left. I wasn't careful about your instructions."

"I see," Dad said. "But at least we found each other. And if we plan on playing baseball together, you'll need these shoes."

I Wonder . . .
I wonder if you can think of a time when you forgot about God, but he didn't let go of you . . .

Even if we are not faithful, he will remain faithful.

2 Timothy 2:13a

Feed My Sheep
John 21:1-17

Do you have a habit of praying each time you sit down to a meal? Mealtime is a good time to remember God, because one of God's great blessings—food—is right in front of you. You can thank God for the food and also pray for friends, family, and people with special needs. You have three times a day to be aware of God.

Jesus loved Peter. And Jesus asked if Peter loved him. Three times Jesus asked. Three times he made Peter think. Each time he asked Peter to do something to prove it—feed Jesus' sheep. Jesus was asking Peter to show his love by taking care of others for Jesus.

If you pray three times today and tell Jesus that you love him, think about how you show it.

Song for the Week:
"If You Love Me," *Songs for LiFE* 151

Prayer for the Week:
Jesus, have I told you that I love you?
Have I told you through friends who need me?
Have I told you through caring about my neighbors?
Have I told you through giving to those in need throughout the world?
Jesus, I love you.
I want to tell you,
and I want to *show* you. Amen.

The Poster

Drew Barna's favorite place at the library was the community bulletin board. He couldn't read all the words on the posters, but usually there were enough pictures to help him. One time he found Kara Merton's kitten, Snuggles, after she put up a missing kitten poster. He fed the black-and-white kitten, then returned it to her.

On Saturday there was a new poster added to the others. He studied words at the top of the poster. For sure one word said PICNIC. But why was there a poster about a picnic? At the bottom of the poster was a picture of a boy who had the same kind of hair and eyes as Drew Barna did. He had never seen anyone look so much like him. Maybe that meant he was supposed to go to the picnic.

A man who walked with a cane and wore suspenders to hold up his gray slacks joined Drew at the bulletin board. "I suppose you're going to the Korean Barbecue Picnic," the man said, tapping the poster with his cane.

Korean. Mom Barna had told him about his country, Korea.

"I was born in Korea," Drew said. "I lived in an orphanage until I came to America. But now I'm American, not Korean."

"Well, the picnic is for Korean-Americans," said the man, "and I'd think that'd be you."

Korean and American. Could he be both? He had to find out.

I Wonder ...
I wonder what you know about yourself—what does it mean to belong to your parents and belong to God . . .

So keep a clear mind. Control yourselves. Then you can pray.

1 Peter 4:7

Kim Chee, Jap Chae, and Bi Bim Nyang

After the man left, Drew touched the picture of the boy.

Kara Merton stopped by the bulletin board. She tacked up a baby-sitting ad.

"Do you think I'm Korean?" Drew asked.

Kara looked at the poster. Then she looked at Drew. "Yes, I'd say so."

"Is that good or bad?" Drew asked.

Kara smiled. "I think Korean is a fine thing to be." She leaned over to read the poster. "This picnic is to raise money for starving children in North Korea. It costs ten dollars per person."

Drew always wanted Mom to tell him the part of his story where the Barna family came to get him at the airport. And how they all thought he was a beautiful baby. He didn't like the part about his Korean family giving him away because there were too many mouths to feed in their family. But he had never thought about other Koreans, and especially not hungry children.

"They're serving Kim Chee, Jap Chae, and Bi Bim Nyang," Kara said. "Do you know what that is?"

"No," Drew said, "I don't know much about being Korean. If I went to the picnic, I could find out. But I can't go by myself, and there are too many Barnas to buy ten-dollar picnic tickets."

I Wonder . . .

I wonder if knowing just a little bit about the needs of North Koreans makes Drew care more about them . . .

Most of all, love one another deeply.

1 Peter 4:8

Chopsticks

God's gifts of grace come in many forms.

1 Peter 4:10a

"What's your poster about?" Drew asked.

"To advertise my services as a baby-sitter. It's a great way to earn money, because I like kids."

"Korean kids too?"

Kara laughed. Then she was quiet. Drew wondered if she was going to say that Korean kids didn't matter so much.

"Drew," Kara said. "Would you like to go to the picnic? I mean with me. I have enough money to pay for both of us."

"You'd do that?"

"It'd be fun; besides, I never gave you a reward for finding Snuggles."

Kara promised to pick Drew up on Saturday morning. Then they looked up North Korea in the encyclopedia while waiting for Mrs. Barna to come for Drew.

The next day Drew practiced eating with a pair of chopsticks that Kara had brought over for him. At breakfast he ate pancakes, toast, and eggs with his chopsticks. At lunch he ate his sandwich and banana with chopsticks. And at suppertime Mrs. Barna fixed rice just so Drew could practice using his chopsticks.

On Saturday morning, Drew was hungry. Eating with chopsticks had slowed him down yesterday. He had spent more time working the chopsticks than actually eating.

I Wonder . . .

I wonder why Drew tried so hard to use the chopsticks . . .

Hungry and Handsome

It was 11 o'clock when Kara walked up to the Barna house. Drew was out of the door before she could ring the doorbell.

"Are you hungry for noodles and beef with vegetables?" she asked.

"Mom told me they might have barbecue chicken," Drew said. "That's my favorite food, right after fried chicken."

Kara took a small notebook out of her pocket. "Dak-Gu-I. That's slices of chicken in a spicy sauce. It's cooked over a grill. You'll like it. But you don't have to try everything. Kim Chee is spicy, pickled cabbage. It might be very different."

"If Koreans eat it, so will I," Drew said. "Do you really think eating all this food is going to help starving children?"

Kara took her twenty dollars out of her pocket. "It's the money that will help."

Drew reached for Kara's hand. "Thank you, Kara."

Drew smelled the picnic before he could see it. He heard the voices too. He felt the kind of excitement he felt at Christmastime.

A North Korean flag, a South Korean flag, and an American flag blew in the breeze next to a platform. Kara and Drew sat on the grass close to the front. Drew noticed more brown-eyed kids with lighted-skinned parents. A proud feeling filled Drew. He didn't feel different like he sometimes did at school. He felt handsome.

I Wonder . . .

I wonder if you know the feeling of being different in some way from people around you . . .

> Each of you has received a gift in order to serve others. You should use it faithfully.
>
> *1 Peter 4:10b*

American and Korean

A young man held a microphone in his hand. "Welcome," he said. "Tens of thousands of Korean children have been adopted over the past thirty years. I was one of them twenty years ago."

Drew turned around. He noticed Korean people of all sizes and ages. Then he whispered to Kara, "I used to think that all kids had dark hair and brown eyes, but parents had blue eyes."

"How funny," Kara said. "Why would you think that?"

Drew blushed. "That's the way it is at our house. Well, at least until Ellie came."

They listened to the man again. "Floods and years of poor crops have left little food for the North Koreans. For some, all there is to eat is grass, tree bark, and roots."

Smells of spicy chicken cooking over small grills caused Drew's stomach to be hungrier than before. He looked down at the grass. His stomach wasn't begging for grass. And for sure not roots or bark from the tree.

He was glad that he was both Korean and American. Korean so he could have something special in his heart that loved people across an ocean. And American so that he could be part of the Barna family who loved him.

I Wonder . . .

I wonder how you can love people who live far away from you . . .

If you serve, you should do it with the strength God provides. Then in all things God will be praised through Jesus Christ.

1 Peter 4:11b

Be sure to check page 250 for more of the story.

Jesus Goes Back to Heaven

Matthew 28:16-18; Acts 1:1-11

Do you ever dream about places you'd like to visit? Maybe you have pictures of these places. Or perhaps your friends have been there and told you how wonderful it is.

Have you ever dreamed about going to heaven? There are no photographs of heaven, and we can't travel there like we do to places on the earth. But Jesus promised that someday we could be there with him. Can you imagine what kind of home the Creator of the stars, moon, and earth has in heaven? It has been described as having streets of gold and gates of pearl. It must be more beautiful and exciting than we can begin to imagine.

But until you get there, Jesus is already in heaven looking after you.

Song for the Week:
"Rejoice, the Lord Is King," *Songs for LiFE* 180

Prayer for the Week:
Sometimes I wonder about your wonderful place
    called heaven.
Will I like it?
What will I be doing there?
Then I think about your gifts to me now,
and I know that your gifts in
    heaven will be
brighter and greater. And I'll
    get to see you.
That sounds awesome.
    Thank you. Amen.

A Dream

Mrs. Love, the first-grade teacher, gave the class an assignment. Everyone had to draw a picture of their house.

Jennifer Jordan drew a small window in a tall building. It was one window in the big apartment building where she lived. If only she lived in a house with a porch and pretty curtains at each window.

She leaned over in her chair so she could see Lucas Barna's picture. Lucas had a face in every window in his house. There were more windows and more faces than even the Barnas had.

"It's my house in heaven," Lucas said as Jennifer counted the windows.

That gave Jennifer an idea. If Lucas could draw a heaven house so could she. The house next to Lucas's was her favorite. It was special enough to be in heaven. Often she dreamed about rocking in the chairs on the wide porch.

So she turned her paper over. This time she was excited as she drew.

Marisa, her stepsister, said that the Ingels lived there. And sometimes they invited kids from the neighborhood over for cookies. Jennifer had never been invited. People didn't tend to notice Jennifer.

Then she had an idea. After school was over, she'd see if the Ingels would come out and invite her in to share all the wonderful things that must be inside that house.

I Wonder . . .
I wonder if you have ever dreamed about an invitation to a special place . . .

Then Christ will live in your hearts because you believe in him.

Ephesians 3:17

Disappointment

Jennifer figured that if she made a quick trip to the Ingels she'd never be missed. Marisa was always busy talking to the other kids on the way home—too busy to notice a little stepsister.

So she crossed the school yard in the opposite direction from home. When she reached the clump of trees in the Ingels's yard, she found a cozy spot where she could watch the house.

A three-colored cat leaped across the yard and right into Jennifer's lap. It snuggled down and purred loudly.

"Pinecone, where are you?" called the lady from the house.

"You must be Pinecone," Jennifer whispered to the cat. "Could you tell the lady I'd like to come inside with you?"

"Pinecone," the lady called again.

The cat jumped off of Jennifer's lap and ran to the lady. Then they slipped though the beautiful front door that had glass of many colors in its window. The door closed. Jennifer sat under the new green leaves of the trees for a long time, hoping that the door would open again and her name would be called.

The May sun ducked behind a cloud. Jennifer shivered. A light went on inside the house. She picked up her schoolbag and walked home.

I Wonder . . .
I wonder how Jennifer can get an invitation to go inside . . .

May you have power with all God's people to understand Christ's love.

Ephesians 3:18a

Heaven?

Jennifer ran home. Marisa was waiting at the door.

"Don't be so poky again," Marisa said. "We promised Mom we'd have the apartment cleaned before she came home."

As Jennifer stacked newspapers and brought empty glasses to the kitchen, she decided this wasn't heaven. But what was heaven? Was it a beautiful place? And who would go to heaven? She couldn't even get an invitation to the place she thought would be the closest to heaven.

She tried to pretend that tomorrow would be different. But she couldn't even make her dreams work that night when she went to bed.

The next morning as she walked into her classroom, she saw the pictures on the bulletin board next to the coat cubbies

"What is that?" Caleb Henry asked, pointing to her picture. "I know you don't live in a house like that."

"It's my house in heaven," Jennifer said.

"Well, you shouldn't make us think it is your house," Caleb said. "Because liars don't go to heaven."

Jennifer wanted to say something about Lucas's picture, but she didn't. Caleb was probably right about liars not going to heaven.

I Wonder . . .
I wonder what you think heaven will be like . . .

May you know how wide and long and high and deep it is. [God's love]

Ephesians 3:18b

An Invitation

Jennifer told her stepsister, Marisa, that she had to stay after school. It felt like another lie. So she quickly told Marisa that she had to look up something for a school paper. That was kind of true.

She hoped Pinecone would be outside so she could get an invitation when Pinecone was called.

But it was quiet outside the house. She walked up to the front door. The sun shone on the colored glass. A basket of flowers in the same colors sat on the step. She almost walked away. But she'd probably never get to heaven if she didn't ask the lady if this house could be her heaven house.

She tapped on the door. Then she squeezed her hands and eyes shut.

The door opened. The grandmother lady with the crown of white hair stood in front of her.

"I—I'm trying to get to heaven," she finally said. It felt as if it came out all wrong.

"Well," said the lady, "perhaps you've come to the right place. I'm Ada Ingel. What is your name?"

"Jennifer."

"Jennifer, that is a beautiful name," Ada Ingel said. "Are you allowed to come inside and have tea and a cookie with me?"

I Wonder . . .

I wonder why this might be the right place for Jennifer to find out about heaven . . .

God is able to do far more than we could ever ask or imagine.

Ephesians 3:20a

The One with Power

Jennifer followed Ada into the house. She took a deep breath. There was a blue-patterned rug on a shiny wooden floor. The curtains were as beautiful as she had imagined. They puffed over the sides of the windows like clouds.

And a sweet, warm smell filled the house.

"I just baked cookies," Ada said. "Would you like to join me for tea?"

Jennifer sat down on the soft cushion of a big wooden chair. While Ada went to get the tea and cookies, Jennifer wondered if heaven was as nice as this. A large, glass bowl sat on the table. Colored marbles filled the bottom of the bowl. They must be worth a lot because no one would keep marbles in such a fancy bowl unless they were valuable.

Ada returned with a plate of cinnamon-sprinkled cookies and tea in bright blue and yellow cups. "Do you like the marbles?" she asked.

Jennifer nodded.

"They belonged to my boy William. But now he's in heaven with God."

"He must have been a very good boy to get to heaven," Jennifer said. "He probably never lied or anything."

Ada laughed. "Sometimes he was naughty. But he knew a very important person who is in charge in heaven and who is in charge on earth too."

Jennifer put down her teacup. "Maybe I can meet that person too."

I Wonder . . .
I wonder what Ada will tell Jennifer . . .

He does everything by his power that is working in us.

Ephesians 3:20b

Wind and Fire on Pentecost

Acts 2

Have you ever walked against a strong wind? Sometimes it feels as if a wall of giant marshmallows is pushing against you—almost pushing you over backwards. The opposite happens if the wind is behind you. If you are on your bike, you might be able to go faster than you've ever gone before. If you are walking, it might seem as if the wind is picking you up right off your feet.

The wind is powerful. If you have felt or seen its force, you know that.

But God wants you to also know that he is powerful. And if his Holy Spirit is living in you, powerful things can happen. The disciples found that out. And so can you.

Song for the Week:
"O Holy Spirit, Breathe on Me," *Songs for LiFE* 183

Prayer for the Week:
I can hear the wind blowing.
I can feel it too.
But how can I feel and hear the Holy Spirit?
Let me know the power of the Holy Spirit
by loving when I don't have love,
by being joyful when
I have an ordinary day.
Let me know the Holy Spirit's power
of love, joy, and peace. Amen.

Special Shoes

"**N**o more," Keely Merton said, dragging a large cardboard box into the bedroom she shared with her younger sister, Kalle. "We are getting rid of all the junk in this room."

"I don't see any junk," Kalle said.

Keely picked up a pair of gray sneakers that used to be white. She dropped them into the box.

"Give those back," Kalle said. "Those are my special sneakers." She pulled out the sneakers. Then, with the laces tied together, she dangled the shoes over a picture on the wall.

"Don't be ridiculous," Keely said. "You can't decorate our room with old shoes."

"Mrs. Ingel does," Kalle said. "She has a pair of shoes on her wall that are seventy years old. Those shoes are her prize possession."

Keely glared at Kalle. "I don't believe you."

"If it isn't true, you may throw away anything of mine that you want," Kalle said.

The girls shook hands on the deal. Then they walked over to Mrs. Ingel's house.

"Show her Johanna's shoes," Kalle said when Mrs. Ingel opened the front door.

"Right there," Mrs. Ingel said, pointing to a living-room wall. "Johanna traveled from village to village in Africa wearing those shoes. Because of her, many Africans heard about Jesus for the first time."

I Wonder . . .
I wonder if there's something in your house that reminds you of Jesus when you look at it . . .

Every day the Lord added to their group those who were being saved.

Acts 2:47b

Fights and Arguments

"See," Kalle said. "She did all that important work wearing those shoes." Keely went over to touch the shoes. "Johanna's shoes are made of beautiful brown leather. They're not ugly shoes like yours."

Kalle stomped her feet. "I do important work in my shoes too. Someday you'll be glad to have my shoes on your wall."

"Yeah, so what do you do that's as important as being a missionary?"

"Girls," Mrs. Ingel said. "I think both of you should sit down on the sofa. One on each end. And I will tell you a story about Johanna.

"One day four African men were helping Johanna. But soon they began to fight. So she led them into her hut. She asked them to sit on the floor away from each other. They weren't allowed to talk until she gave them permission. This gave them time to cool down. Johanna glared at them while she drank her tea. Finally the four men were ready to apologize and pray together."

The girls looked sideways at each other. They didn't say anything.

Mr. Ingel came into the room. He rubbed his white hair when he saw the girls. "Why the long faces?" he asked.

"I can't be like the missionary Johanna because of my sister," Kalle said.

I Wonder . . .
I wonder what is really keeping Kalle from being like Johanna . . .

At one time you were far away from God. But now you belong to Christ Jesus. He spilled his blood for you. That has brought you near to God.

Ephesians 2:13

Another African Story

"Hmm." Mr. Ingel pulled off his glasses. "I have an idea. Kalle, run upstairs to my office. Find my notebook of missionary letters and bring them down here."

When Kalle returned with the map-covered notebook, Mr. Ingel flipped through the pages. "Here's a good story," he said.

"Muslim leaders in a certain African country were desperate. Too many Muslims were becoming Christians."

"I bet there are many Christians in Africa because of the work of missionaries like Johanna," Kalle said.

"That's right," Mr. Ingel said. "Including Ali. Before he became a Christian, he was an important Muslim leader in his village. After he started trusting Jesus, he was hated and put into prison."

"Did he ask God to get rid of his enemies?" Keely asked.

"No," Mr. Ingel said. "Ali and the other believers who were in prison prayed for those who brought them so much trouble. They said, 'Lord, forgive their sins. Wash them. Make them whiter than cotton.'"

Kalle pulled up her socks. No matter how much dirt she got into, her mother always made sure she had clean, white, cotton socks. It was nice to be clean. How could Ali wish something so good for those who hated him?

I Wonder . . .
I wonder if you ever find it hard to wish good things for someone who doesn't treat you fairly . . .

Christ himself is our peace.

Ephesians 2:14a

A Fiery Cross

"Let me tell you about the kind of people who were after Ali," Mr. Ingel said. "One of them was a man named Bradi. He was known as a tough man. When the Muslims wanted to get rid of someone, they'd call on Bradi and his crew. So the Muslims gave Bradi Ali's name. That very night Bradi started repeating curses against Ali."

Kalle shivered.

"In the middle of Bradi's curses, he saw a hand rise up as if to stop him. Then another hand appeared over the first hand to make the sign of the cross. Bradi tried harder with the curses. All through the night he repeated the curses until he had no energy left. Finally he fell asleep.

"While he was sleeping, he had a dream. In the dream he saw three men standing in the distance. A cross stood between him and the three men. Without warning the cross moved toward him. It touched his forehead, and it felt like the hot iron that a cow's owner uses to brand his animals. When Bradi woke up, the men and the cross were gone, but he still felt what seemed like a fiery cross mark on his forehead."

Keely slid across the sofa and sat next to Kalle.

He has destroyed the hatred that was like a wall between us.

Ephesians 2:14c

I Wonder...

I wonder if this dream could remove the hate Bradi had for Christians and especially for Ali . . .

The Man from the Dream

"In the morning, Bradi left the brick house with its zinc roof where he was staying. He asked a friend to show him the prison where he could find Ali.

"He wasn't sure what he'd do, but because of the dream he felt he needed to take a look at Ali. When he saw Ali, he let out a cry.

"Ali was one of the three men he had seen in his dream!

"Bradi's heart was filled with questions about the dream and about the cross. So now he talked eagerly to the man that only yesterday he had meant to destroy. Ali explained the gospel to Bradi.

"Through the truth of Jesus and the power of Ali's love in praying for his enemies, Bradi accepted the gospel."

Mr. Ingel closed his notebook. "We need to pray that God will protect Bradi as he tells Muslims about Jesus. Muslims don't know the message of the cross. They don't know the love of Jesus, God's son, that was so strong that he died on a cross for them."

Kalle wished she could be like Ali. Then she thought of a way to begin.

"Keely," Kalle said, "I don't think we should hang my shoes up on the wall."

"I was just thinking it wouldn't be so bad," Keely said.

Both girls laughed and hugged each other.

I Wonder . . .

I wonder if you have ever shown love to someone who has been mean to you . . .

Through Christ we both come to the Father by the power of one Holy Spirit.

Ephesians 2:18

Be sure to check page 251 for more of the story.

A Man Jumps for Joy

Acts 3:1-16

Make a list of all the kind things you've done lately. You may have even helped someone without knowing you made a difference. Listening to a friend, cooperating in your class at school, and talking to your grandparents on the phone all count.

Now think about why you did these things. Is it possible to say that you did them in the name of Jesus?

Peter and John healed the crippled beggar in the name of Jesus. They knew it was Jesus' love and power in their hearts and hands that made them care about this beggar.

Song for the Week:
"When Did We See You," *Songs for LiFE* 245

Prayer for the Week:
My hands are busy all the time.
But are they busy because I love you, Jesus?
My feet go here and there.
But are they going places because I love you, Jesus?
My mind thinks of hundreds of things every day.
But is it working because I love you, Jesus?
Take all I do and say for your kingdom. Amen.

Caught

Corey Kemp packed his right fist into his baseball glove. Any moment now he expected the batter to hit the ball over to him in center field. He scratched the toe of his shoe in the dirt.

Smack. He heard the whack of the ball against the bat. And it was coming his way. He tracked the ball in the sky. It was coming faster and further than he thought it would from this batter. In seconds he backed up in fast gear.

Faster and faster he ran backwards, keeping eye contact with the ball. Suddenly the heel of his foot hit a hard object. With a crash he tumbled backwards. Two bikes had been dropped at the edge of the baseball field, and now Corey was tangled up between bars and pedals.

A sharp pain ran through his right leg. Then it seemed as if the baseball field was spinning.

"Corey. Corey. Are you okay?"

A dizzy circle of faces appeared above him.

"My leg," he muttered.

He heard more shouts and fuzzy voices. Everyone was pointing to his leg. He forced himself to look too. The bone in his leg had broken through the skin. Help, he thought. Who would help him? Then he couldn't think at all.

I Wonder . . .

I wonder if you've ever felt completely helpless . . . I wonder where God is when you need help . . .

Through faith in Jesus we have received God's grace. In that grace we stand.

Romans 5:2a

Why Me?

Out of nowhere it seemed an ambulance appeared. Strong arms scooped Corey up.

At the hospital voices rushed around him. He wanted help, but it hurt too much—too much for anyone to help. Leave me alone, he wanted to shout when they lifted him onto a table. Then he screamed inside as the doctor worked on his leg.

Why did this have to happen? Those little kids with their bikes needed to stay away from the baseball field.

"Corey," said his mother, gently rubbing his head after the doctor had finished. "Timothy Bennett and Zachary Wit are here. It was their bikes that you tripped over. They came to say they're sorry."

Corey turned his head away from his mom.

"Corey," she said softly.

Hot tears streamed across his face, down onto his neck, and soaked into the paper sheeting on the table. "Tell them to go away," he said.

"Well, young man," the doctor said, "when you break a leg, you sure make a thorough job of it. I have some pills for you to take for the pain. But promise me no more wrestling with bikes."

As a nurse helped him into the wheelchair, Corey stared at his huge, white, casted leg as straight as a baseball bat. But that leg wouldn't be out on the baseball field this spring.

I Wonder . . .

I wonder if anything good can come out of Corey's bad break . . .

We are full of joy even when we suffer. We know that our suffering gives us the strength to go on.

Romans 5:3b

The Comics

At home, Corey stared up at the ceiling from his bed. He had told his mom he didn't want anything—no visitors, nothing—just his door closed.

Now he was sorry he had been such a grouch. The pain pill was starting to work, and he wished he had his comic books. Maybe later he'd ask his mom to get them.

At least he had his computer. Only last week he had moved the desk next to his bed. He had rigged it up so that he could bring the keyboard over to the bed. The mouse pad could sit alongside him on the bed.

What if he did a comic book search on the Internet? Corey forgot about his troubles as he waited for his search to come up with a new way to tune into his favorite pastime.

First he found a listing called Hot Stuff. It had comics created by many different people. Corey thought it'd be great to learn to do that.

But right now he felt like finding Superman. He went down the list—Superman in Bosnia. That'd be worth checking.

He clicked on the heading. The article reported that a half a million Superman comic books were sent to the country of Bosnia. The comics were written to teach kids about the dangers of land mines. The sample on the screen showed a picture of a boy leaning on crutches. While playing in a park near his home, he had stepped on a land mine. The exploding mine burned him and shredded the bone in his leg. As a result his leg had to be removed.

I Wonder . . .

I wonder what went through Corey's mind when he read about the boy in Bosnia . . .

Land Mines

Corey's stomach rolled uncomfortably as he thought about the boy with no leg. But he liked the part of the story where Superman rescued two Bosnian boys from a minefield. And he was glad Superman could teach the boys how to avoid risky places and look out for possible hidden mines.

But what exactly were land mines?

Corey returned to the beginning to do another search. This time he typed in "land mines." Land mines, he read, were left behind from wars. The mines were hidden underground or camouflaged by leaves and bushes. Even though it cost only a few dollars to place them there, it cost thousands to remove them. And at the rate they were being removed, it'd take over fifty years to get rid of them all. He read on—10 million land mines were buried in Cambodia, 3-6 million in Bosnia, and 15 million in Angola. It was too hard to even imagine so many hidden traps.

Sometimes the mines exploded on children playing outside their homes. And farmers couldn't plant in their fields because of the mines. So the people in these countries faced great food shortages.

Further down on the screen was a man showing a poster to a group of kids. More pictures—this time a boy from Angola who was learning to walk with an artificial leg.

Corey let the mouse drop to his side. A message on his screen asked him if he wanted to continue. He didn't respond. The program shut itself down. He thought about the Superman comic. At least something was being done. But what could he do?

I Wonder . . .

I wonder what makes you understand the pain of others . . .

God has poured his love into our hearts.

Romans 5:5b

A Way to Help

"Corey." His mom came into the room. "Can I get you anything? The phone has been ringing all afternoon. You've had offers of hamburger meals and comic books."

"Did Timothy and Zachary call back?" Corey asked.

"About every ten minutes," his mom said. "They're very sorry about this."

Corey thought about the land mines. He couldn't explain it, but he wasn't angry at the boys anymore. It was an accident. What he was angry about were the kids who were hurt in the land mines. They were hurt because no one cared.

"I'd like Timothy and Zachary to come over," he said.

"I'll call them now," Corey's mom said.

Within five minutes, the boys were standing at Corey's bedside. They looked scared until Corey asked them to sign his cast with a marker pen.

"You could be a beggar," Timothy said.

"Yeah," Zachary said. "Like the lame man we had in our Bible story on Sunday."

Corey pulled himself to sit up straight. "You're right. Go and tell everyone to bring me the money they'd spend on hamburgers and magazines for cheering me up."

"You don't really have to be a beggar," Timothy said. "I was joking."

"I know," Corey said, "but in this case money will give me the chance to help some kids."

I Wonder . . .
I wonder what caused Corey to change . . .

He did it [poured out his love] through the Holy Spirit, whom he has given to us.

Romans 5:5c

Be sure to check page 252 for more of the story.

Punished for Preaching
Acts 5:12-42

If your friends want to play tag, but you want to jump rope, what do you do? Or if your family wants to rent a video, but you want to play board games, what happens? You may end up by yourself. And if you really like what you are doing, that may be okay. It can be fun to be a little bit different.

But what if your choice to be different meant that others would make it hard for you. What would you do? Sometimes that's what happens when people decide to follow Jesus. That choice can make those who don't understand about Jesus very angry.

Choosing Jesus is not like any other choice, because belonging to Jesus changes you forever. You can't go back to the old ways. Even if you face punishment, hurt, and teasing, the love for Jesus will keep you strong. It's a forever kind of love!

Song for the Week:
"Standing on the Lord's Side,"
Songs for LiFE 227

Prayer for the Week:
Jesus, I want to stand on your side.
Thank you for making that easy for me.
Help those who may find themselves
    in trouble
because they stand for you.
Make them strong against their enemies.
And make me always strong for you
    too. Amen.

Different

anell Ingel hugged her dad goodbye and hurried out of the car so she could spend the day with her Grandpa Ingel. On Wednesdays she studied about maps and people from around the world. Grandpa had traveled all over so he knew many things.

"There goes that girl who doesn't go to school," said a boy who was walking toward Credo Canyon School.

"Yeah, she must be pretty dumb," said another boy.

Janell held her violin case against her body and quickly ran to her grandfather's porch. Why couldn't other kids understand that with her music schedule, it worked better to be home-schooled?

Grandpa opened the door for her. "Today we have a special treat," he said. "Sophie TenBerg is coming over. She is having tea with us and telling us about Japan."

Janell had seen Sophie TenBerg before at the grocery store. Sophie wore sandals with socks that separated at the toe to fit into the sandals. She was very different.

Right now Janell didn't want to be a part of anything that was different.

"I want you to do what Sophie does," Grandpa said. "That way you'll learn about Japanese ways."

Janell stashed her violin behind the sofa. She wanted to ask Grandpa if they could have a new plan. One where she'd learn the same things as the kids who went to school.

I Wonder . . .
I wonder how it makes you feel to be different from others around you . . .

We know that in all things God works for the good of those who love him.

Romans 8:28a

Unusual Ways

Before Janell could say anything, Sophie came to the door.

"Isn't she early?" Janell asked.

"In Japan it's better to be early than late," Grandpa said.

Janell liked being early too. Now she was curious. What else would Sophie do?

The first thing Sophie did was bow. Her feet were together, and her hands were at her sides. After she bowed to Grandpa, she bowed to Janell.

Janell wasn't sure what to do, so she bent her head down. It wasn't the same as Sophie's bow from the waist, but Janell thought at least she tried.

Next, while still facing Grandpa and Janell, Sophie took off her sandals. Then she carefully placed them by the front door with the sandal toes pointing toward the door.

"Should I put my shoes by the door like hers?" Janell whispered to Grandpa.

"No," Grandpa said. "She is doing that because she is a guest. The shoes pointing toward the door show that her shoes are ready when it's time for her to leave."

"I'll call you when the tea is prepared," Sophie said, leaving for the kitchen.

"Now when Sophie calls us," Grandpa said, "don't sit down until Sophie asks."

"There is so much to learn," Janell said. "Wouldn't it be better if all people were the same?"

I Wonder . . .

I wonder why Sophie, who was a missionary to Japan, was careful to learn the ways of the Japanese people . . .

God planned that those he had chosen would become like his Son.

Romans 8:29

Strong Tea

Grandpa pulled out Janell's violin case. He opened it and took out the violin. "This is a beautiful instrument," he said, gliding his hand across the smooth wood. "But if I'd play it, it'd sound terrible."

"Oh, Grandpa," Janell said. "If you could play songs, then you wouldn't want to listen to me playing."

"That's why I'm glad we're not all the same," Grandpa said.

Janell noticed the twinkle in Grandpa's eyes. Then she took both of his hands and danced with him. "You're right," she said. "Thank you for inviting Sophie."

When Sophie came into the room, she wore a long, shiny, colorful robe.

She invited everyone to sit. Then she poured tea into small cups without handles. With both hands she passed the cup of tea to Janell.

"Take it with both hands," whispered Grandpa. "That's the Japanese way."

Janell thought about the way she took both of Grandpa's hands earlier. She loved Grandpa so much that one hand didn't seem enough. So with both hands she took the tea from Sophie.

"You can slurp it a bit," Sophie said. "A very soft slurp shows you appreciate it."

Janell giggled. She slurped the tea. It had a strong taste. She tried another slurp. It tasted better.

I Wonder...

I wonder what difference it made to the Japanese people that Sophie learned their ways . . .

Stronger Than Tea

When Sophie set her cup down, Janell set hers down too.

"Do you like to do everything the Japanese way?" Janell asked.

Sophie poured Janell another cup of tea. "I wanted the Japanese people to be comfortable with me, and I wanted to be comfortable with them, so I learned their ways."

"Tell me more," Janell said.

"First I must tell you that all people need to be changed," Sophie said. "The kind of change that happens because of God's love. It is the most powerful thing we can know. But being changed by God's love doesn't fit easily into the Japanese way. When you are changed, it makes you different. And being different isn't easy in Japan."

"It isn't easy here, either," Janell said.

Sophie reached for Janell's hands. They held hands across the table. "In Japan everyone is expected to worship 80 million different gods. A Japanese Christian who believes that Jesus is the only way to salvation is sticking out from the group."

"Can't the Japanese people just hide their love for Jesus in their hearts?" Janell asked.

"Michiko was a young girl like you," Sophie said. "She loved Jesus and wanted to belong completely to him, so she asked to be baptized. Her parents were against it. They didn't want their daughter to be different. On the Sunday morning that she was to be baptized, Michiko did not come to church. I never saw her again."

I Wonder . . .

I wonder if Michiko is separated from God now . . .

I'm absolutely sure that not even death or life can separate us from God's love.

Romans 8:38a

Hope

Janell gripped Sophie's hands tighter. "Does that happen every time?"

"No," Sophie said. "There is better news in some cases. Hirotsugu Mochida was twelve years old when he heard about Jesus on a radio program. The news of Jesus touched his heart. Hiro could not forget what he heard. Four years later he knew he wanted to make a decision to accept Jesus. His parents were very upset. They thought their son was disobedient towards them. He was forced to choose between his family and Jesus. He chose Jesus."

"It was a good choice," Janell whispered.

"Yes, it was," Sophie said. "Today he is a believer. He shares his faith with others too. There are nearly fifty thousand people in his neighborhood. He meets with as many people as possible and tells them the good news of Jesus Christ."

"I hope I can always be brave about being on Jesus' side," Janell said. "But I'm afraid I might not be. Before you came, I didn't even feel brave about being different from the kids who go to school."

"It's okay," Sophie said. "None of us can be brave by ourselves."

Janell nodded. She felt the silky skin of Sophie's touch. Could Jesus be as close to her as Sophie was right now? If Hiro could know that, so could she.

I Wonder . . .
I wonder if it was easy for Hiro to decide about Jesus . . .

Nothing at all can ever separate us from God's love because of what Christ Jesus our Lord has done.

Romans 8:39b

Be sure to check page 253 for more of the story.

Philip and the Ethiopian

Acts 8:26-39

It can happen on a desert road in a chariot, or it can happen on the playground under the crossbars. It can happen in North America, Africa, or Honduras. God can plan for anyone to meet one of his believers.

This is how it happened in Honduras one day.

John Wind, a pastor working in Tegucigalpa, Honduras, for Christian Reformed World Missions, went to the store to do some errands. A young man came up to him.

"Excuse me, sir. Are you a pastor?" asked the young man, Armando.

Pastor Wind realized that this young man had noticed the Christian books he was carrying. "Yes, I am," Pastor Wind said.

"I've been asking God to send me a person like you to talk to. I'm very confused right now," Armando said.

Armando is a new believer, and Pastor Wind is there to help Armando know the ways of God. Next time it could be you that God sends to help someone know of his great love and salvation.

Song for the Week:
"You and I," *Songs for LiFE* 246, stanzas 1, 2, and 3

Prayer for the Week:
There are hearts that are ready to hear about you. Help me know when someone is calling for you and what I can tell them about you. Amen.

Unexpected News

Peter Wit couldn't wait for supper to be over. His best friend, Trevor, had given him a secret coded message. As soon as he decoded it, he'd know where to meet Trevor.

It wasn't his turn to help with dishes, so after supper he scooted toward his room.

"Peter," said Mr. Wit, "come into the study with me. I want to talk with you."

His dad sounded serious. Was something wrong?

Slowly Peter followed his dad to the study. He sat in the chair across from his dad.

"I have a decision to make," his dad said. "My company wants to transfer me to another job site. If I say yes, we'd have to move two hundred miles across the state."

Peter thought about the secret code. It wasn't made for long distance. "Well, I think you should say no," Peter said.

"I'm thinking about saying no," Mr. Wit said. "But if I do, it's so I can join a team of Bible translators."

Everything inside of Peter screeched to a stop. "You mean like the translators we pray for at supper—the ones who work years and years in far-away villages?"

"Yes. Some of them need computer experts right now. We've prayed for them so long because my heart is with them. But maybe now is the time to give them more than my heart."

I Wonder . . .
I wonder what Mr. Wit meant when he said, "Maybe now is the time to give them more than my heart" . . .

Faraway Places

Peter put his finger on the globe that sat on his father's desk. He gave the globe a spin. "Where would we go?"

"It depends where they need me the most. It could be Africa, South America, or an island in the Pacific Ocean."

Peter remembered a picture of a boy they had prayed for in Africa. His hair was braided with beads. And he wore a feather that was attached to the beads. He couldn't imagine that boy being his friend in the place of Trevor. "Can't we just keep on praying for the people?" he asked. "I'd be happy to give more of my allowance."

This time Mr. Wit gave the globe a spin. He stopped the globe when his finger landed on the country of Chile in South America. "Last year we heard the story about the area of Mapuche in Chile. You were so excited about the woman who heard the gospel for the first time in her Mapudungun language."

Peter nodded. "She had heard the gospel in Spanish but never understood it. Then just before she died, she heard it in her language. She asked Jesus into her heart."

"There are almost seven thousand languages in the world," Mr. Wit said.

"And over two-thirds of those languages don't have a single verse of Scripture."

I Wonder . . .
I wonder what you would know about Jesus if you never saw a Bible or heard a word from the Bible . . .

He [God, our Savior] wants everyone to be saved. He wants them to come to know the truth.

1 Timothy 2:4

Sheep and Giraffes

"I remember the first story you told us about translators," Peter said. "It was about sheep and giraffes."

"Oh yes," Mr. Wit said. "That story came from Guatemala. When a non-Spanish-speaking group first received the New Testament in their language, they came together to rejoice. The pastor held up a drawing of a giraffe eating the leaves from a tall tree. A sheep stood beside the giraffe with nothing to eat. "We used to be like the sheep," said the pastor. "We could not reach the food on the tree. The food of God's Word was only for those who could understand Spanish."

Peter walked over to the bookshelf. He counted five different Bibles, but even though they were different, they were all written in English. Sometimes he got stuck reading the long names in the Bible, but otherwise he could read most of it. He even had some favorite verses that he had memorized.

"So will you pray about it?" his dad asked.

"You mean about going faraway?"

His dad nodded.

"What if you get a different answer than I get?" Peter asked.

Mr. Wit put his arm around Peter. "It's a chance we'll have to take. But I think if our whole family is praying, we'll come up with the right answer."

I Wonder . . .
I wonder if it is easy to trust God for the right answer when we pray . . .

There is only one God. And there is only one go-between for God and human beings. He is the man Christ Jesus.

1 Timothy 2:5

Secret Codes

Peter went to his room. He took out the coded message that Trevor had given him. First he checked to see if Trevor had just reversed the alphabet, changing a's into z's and b's into y's. No, that wasn't it.

Trevor was trickier this time. After several tries, Peter figured out that Trevor had moved each letter three letters ahead. Now the a's were represented by d's.

Finally he decoded the message. "Meet me in the apple tree. I'll be sitting on the third limb from the bottom. Trevor."

He hurried outside. The apple tree that grew between their yards was in full bloom. If he didn't know Trevor was up there, he'd never see him through the leaves.

"What took you so long?" Trevor asked. "Get stumped by my code?"

Peter gave his friend a fisted nudge in the arm. "It was a tricky code, but it was my dad who gave me a harder message to figure out."

Trevor was quiet as Peter explained what was happening.

"So what do you think?" Peter asked.

"I—I could never say goodbye to you," Trevor finally said.

"Me either," Peter said.

At 7 o'clock, Trevor's mom called him to come home. The boys changed their secret handshake and made plans to meet before breakfast the next day.

I Wonder . . .

I wonder what makes it so hard for good friends to think about leaving each other . . .

> He [Christ Jesus] gave himself to pay for the sins of everyone.
>
> *1 Timothy 2:6*

E-Mail and Prayer Mail

I want men everywhere to pray. I want them to lift up holy hands.

1 Timothy 2:8

"**W**here's Dad?" Peter asked when he got home.

"On the computer," Zach said.

Dad turned away from the computer screen when Peter entered the office. "I have an e-mail from India," Dad said. "Would you like to read it?"

Peter pulled up a chair beside his dad. He read the message:

For three years Saidulu was unable to walk on his own. He spent his time lying on a bed in a small hut. He had visited witch doctors in the village, but nothing worked. There was no more hope. Then one day a man passed by his hut and tossed in a small booklet. Saidulu pushed it aside, but later he noticed it was written in his language. That was unusual, because his language only belonged to a poor group of people who simply lived off the land wherever they could find food and water.

In this booklet, Saidulu read about a man who also couldn't move off his bed. This man's friends took him to Jesus. And Jesus healed the man. Saidulu prayed to be healed too. All week he prayed. Soon movement began returning to his useless foot.

"I think I hear what you are hearing," Peter said. "People have to hear about Jesus in their own language."

"You have a listening heart," said Mr. Wit.

"And no matter where we go, we can have e-mail," Peter said. "I bet I could learn some great codes in other languages to send to Trevor."

I Wonder . . .

I wonder if you have ever prayed for someone to know about Jesus' salvation . . .

Be sure to check page 254 for more of the story.

Go Tell
Matthew 28:16-20

Gemologists are people who study and collect valuable gems. They might buy green emeralds from Africa, red rubies from Myanmar (Burma), blue sapphires from Cambodia, and purple amethysts from Brazil. They cut the stones from these mines just right to make the colors and sparkles brilliant. Gemologists get excited when they hear about a newly discovered mine somewhere in the world.

Jesus collects gems too. All those who give their hearts to Jesus are like gems. They sparkle and reflect the light of Jesus. All the angels in heaven and all believers get excited when they hear of a new Christian in Peru, Romania, or Chicago.

Wouldn't it be thrilling to hear about more people discovering God? To see people glowing with the love of Jesus?

Song for the Week:
"Shine, Jesus, Shine," *Songs for LiFE* 239

Prayer for the Week:
Jesus, help me spread your good news
around the world.
Let the whole world shine
with your light in our hearts.
Let me start with a prayer.
Let me continue with the way I talk to others,
with the way I spend my money,
and with the way I use my time. Amen.

Missing Words

Trevor pointed his mouse arrow to start his e-mail program. The past three days he had checked for e-mail from Peter, but nothing was there. Either Peter had forgotten about him, or he had better things to do. Well, that wasn't the case for Trevor. He was stuck in Credo Canyon for the summer with nothing fun or important to do.

He counted under his breath while the phone modem went into action. Yes, there was a message, and it was from Peter in Mexico!

"It's hot down here," Peter wrote. "We are all learning Spanish, but I'm not very good at it yet. That makes it interesting to go to the market. So far, I'm very good at pointing and asking for a Coke. Look under the apple tree between our yards. I left you a message written on river rocks."

"Yes!" Peter jumped up from the computer. He ran outside. But before he got to the apple tree, he noticed a moving van in front of Peter's house. The "For Rent" sign was gone. Then Trevor saw a boy run from the apple tree with something in his hands.

Trevor ran to the tree, angry that he didn't get there before this boy discovered Peter's secret message. Two river-rock-sized indents were left in the grass. But one smooth white rock was still there. Trevor turned it over. The word PRAY was written on it. He turned it back over. There was no way he could figure out Peter's message with the other words missing.

I Wonder . . .
I wonder what message Peter wanted to share with his best friend, Trevor . . .

Brandon

"What are you doing under my apple tree?" asked a voice.

Trevor turned to face the boy who he had seen earlier.

"The apple tree is split halfway between your yard and mine," Trevor said.

"So who gets the apples?" the boy asked.

"We share them."

"That's not what the stones said."

But before Trevor could ask what words were on the stones, a woman yelled from the porch. "Brandon, we have more boxes to carry into the house."

The boy ran toward his mother without saying goodbye to Trevor.

More than ever, Trevor missed Peter. The way Brandon had acted, the chances of seeing the other stones weren't good.

Peter crossed the street to get around the moving van. Corey Kemp and Timothy Bennett were sitting on the curb at the corner.

"We prayed for him," Timothy said, holding up a picture of a boy with crutches.

"Now we're going to write him a letter," Corey said.

Corey had become good friends with Timothy after the accident Corey had with Timothy and Zachary's bikes. Timothy must be happy to have a friend after Zach moved. Why couldn't that have happened for me, Trevor thought.

I Wonder . . .

I wonder if you have special things you share with a best friend . . .

> He [God] brought us back to himself through Christ's death on the cross. And he has given us the task of bringing others back to him through Christ.
>
> *2 Corinthains 5:18b*

A Letter from a Friend

"Trevor," called Mr. Ingel from across the street.

Trevor jumped up. It was nice to hear someone calling his name.

"Trevor, I have a stamp for you. It's from Africa. There's a lion on it."

Trevor ran across the street. Two lions were on the stamp. It was the first lion postage stamp he had ever seen.

"Who sent you a letter from Africa?" Trevor asked.

"A friend who works there," Mr. Ingel said. "He teaches the people about Jesus and the Bible."

Mr. Ingel's friend was like Peter—both in places where they could tell someone about Jesus.

"My friend sends me letters, so I know how to pray for him," Mr. Ingel said

"That's what I'd do if Brandon hadn't messed up Peter's prayer message," mumbled Trevor.

"What did you say?" asked Mr. Ingel.

"Nothing," Trevor said. "Tell me about the rest of the letter."

I Wonder . . .

I wonder if you need to be in special, faraway places to tell others about Jesus . . .

So we are Christ's official messengers. It is as if God were making his appeal through us. Here is what Christ wants us to beg you to do. Come back to God!

2 Corinthians 5:20

The Source of Power

Mr. Ingel turned over the page of the letter. "Listen to this. Reuben, one of my friend's young students, now leads his family in devotions. His favorite story is from the book of Acts—the story of the apostle Peter boldly speaking the word of God. Reuben wants the Holy Spirit to be in his life too."

"How can you tell if the Holy Spirit is in your life?" Trevor asked.

"That's a good question," Mr. Ingel said. "Let's read more about Reuben:

> *One day Reuben came home from school. He usually likes to get a snack first. But on this day he thought he'd better quickly pray for his brother.*
>
> *Later he found out that his brother had been hit by a motorbike but wasn't hurt. Now Reuben is thankful that the Holy Spirit urged him to pray for his brother.*

"Wow," Trevor said. "That worked out just right."

"My friend writes that the other ten- and eleven-year-olds in his class talk about the Holy Spirit in their lives too. One boy says the Holy Spirit helps him speak about Jesus to his friends. And another one says the Holy Spirit helps him be kind to his sister."

"The Holy Spirit is a helper then," Trevor said.

Mr. Ingel nodded.

"Thanks for the stamps," Trevor said. "And for telling me about Reuben."

I Wonder . . .

I wonder if the Holy Spirit has ever helped you to show kindness, love, joy, or peace . . .

And take the sword of the Holy Spirit. The sword is God's word.

Ephesians 6:17b

Filling in the Message

Slowly Trevor walked down Stepping Stone Avenue. He touched the PRAY stone in his pocket. Most of his prayers were the same. "Bless this food." "Bless Mom and Dad." They didn't have much to do with talking to others about Jesus.

But he could pray for Peter. Pray that Peter could learn his Spanish and tell all the Spanish-speaking people about Jesus.

The moving van pulled away from curb. Brandon must be moved in now. What a crazy kid—thinking that the apples were only for him. Then Trevor remembered the stones. What if the words on the stones Brandon picked up said "for Brandon"? Suddenly it made sense that that was what the stones *did* say. The message Peter left on the stones was PRAY FOR BRANDON.

Brandon sat on one pile of boxes while opening a box from another pile.

"What's that?" Trevor asked, pointing to a round barrel attached to a small motor.

"That's my rock tumbler," Brandon said. "I like to find interesting rocks. Then I put them in there. The tumbler bounces them around until they are smooth. Sometimes they come out looking valuable."

"The canyon is full of interesting stones," Trevor said. "I could show you."

As a smile spread across Brandon's face, Trevor's hopes for a great summer soared.

I Wonder . . .
I wonder if the Holy Spirit is asking you to pray for anyone . . .

At all times, pray by the power of the Spirit. . . . praying for all of God's people.

Ephesians 6:18

Be sure to check page 255 for more of the story.

Devotion *extras*

More Than a Bag of Rice *extra*

The stories of the needs in Rwanda and Cambodia came from workers with the Christian Reformed World Relief Committee (CRWRC), an organization that helps people wherever the need arises. You can make a difference with them through your prayers and money.

Ask how you can help a family in need through CRWRC's *Free A Family* program.

CRWRC—United States
2850 Kalamazoo Ave. SE
Grand Rapids, MI 49560-0600

CRWRC—Canada
P.O. Box 5070, STN LCD 1
Burlington, ON L7R 3Y8

Never an End *extra*

The story about Rosita is true. Christian doctors working through the Luke Society in Honduras found Rosita begging on the streets.

The Luke Society helps connect doctors and volunteers to those who need help. They work to keep people healthy in many parts of the world. You can find out more about the Luke Society and the people they help by checking to see if your church gets their newsletters or by writing to them.

The Luke Society
P.O. Box 349
Vicksburg, MS 39181

American and Korean *extra*

UNICEF was one organization that provided food and vaccines for children in North Korea. They work worldwide to help children.

UNICEF
United Nations Children's Fund
333 East 38th St.
New York, NY 10016
Tel. 212-686-5522

Needs around the world change because of disasters and leadership in countries. You can find out about current needs by contacting InterAction. This is a group of more than 150 nonprofit organizations working worldwide. It leads the U.S. in caring for the world's poor.

InterAction
1717 Massachusetts Ave. NW
Suite 801
Washington, DC 20036
Tel. 202-687-8227
Web Site: http://www.interaction.org
E-mail: ia@interaction.org

The Man from the Dream *extra*

The story of Johanna is from the true story of Johanna Veenstra, one of the first Reformed missionaries in Africa.

> Zandstra, Gerald L. *Daughters Who Dared* (Calvin Theological Seminary and CRC Publications, 1992), pp. 37-38.

The story of Ali and Bradi is a true story from Africa today. Real names and sources are not given to protect those still involved in this situation.

Pray for missionaries and Christians in Africa.

Find out more about missions in Africa from your church. The number of Christians continues to grow on that continent and the Holy Spirit has filled many with enthusiasm for the gospel, but the difficulties are also great.

You can find out more from these missionary organizations:

RCA Mission Services
4500 60th St. SE
Grand Rapids, MI 49512
Web Site: http://www.rca.org

Christian Reformed World Missions
2850 Kalamazoo Ave. SE
Grand Rapids, MI 49560
Web Site: http://www.crcna.org

A Way to Help *extra*

UNICEF worked with the U.S. government and DC Comics to send Superman comics and information packets to schools in Bosnia. This information informed kids about the land mines and warned them about returning to their old playing fields even after they appeared to be peaceful.

World Vision, an organization dedicated to helping children around the world, has also helped children affected by land mines. They have educated people about the dangers of land mines. They have provided for the needs of those already injured and have brought the good news of Jesus.

UNICEF
United Nations Children's Fund
333 East 38th St.
New York, NY 10016
Tel. 212-686-5522

World Vision
P.O. Box 78481
Tacoma, WA 98481-8481
Web Site: http://www.worldvision.org

Hope *extra*

The story of Michiko is a true story, although that is not her real name. Michiko's real name needs to be protected to prevent any persecution from her family.

The story of Hirotsugu Moichida is also true, and that is his real name. Now he is the pastor of the Misato Reformed Church in Japan.

Hirotsugu Moichida first heard the gospel presented by *The Back to God Hour*, a radio ministry of the Christian Reformed Church.

Perhaps your church supports a missionary in Japan. Pray for him or her and for all who work to bring the gospel to the Japanese people.

You can find out more about missions in Japan through

RCA Mission Services
4500 60th St. SE
Grand Rapids, MI 49512
Web Site: www.rca.org.

Christian Reformed World Missions
2850 Kalamazoo Ave. SE
Grand Rapids, MI 49560
Web Site: www.crcna.org.

E-Mail and Prayer Mail *extra*

The Mapuche woman in Chile was able to hear the gospel in her own language as the result of Wycliffe translators.

The pastor in Guatemala who told the story of the sheep and the giraffe also was rejoicing because of the work of Wycliffe translators.

The story of Saidulu in India resulted from the work of International Bible Society, whose goal is to provide Bibles in many languages. Saidulu was soon baptized, and because he was now a new person, he also wanted a new name. He is now known by the name Isaac, and he brings the good news of Jesus Christ to all his people.

Wycliffe members work directly with groups of people who speak over a thousand different languages. Together they translate Scripture into these languages. Some language groups are as small as fifty people and some groups number in the millions.

The International Bible Society plans to work with Wycliffe Bible Translators to provide New Testaments in fifty different languages for the first time and to provide single books of the Bible in one hundred and fifty languages for the first time.

For more information about Wycliffe, write

Wycliffe Bible Translators
P.O. Box 2727
Huntington Beach, CA 92647
Tel. 1-800-Wycliffe (1-800-992-5433)
Web Site: www.wycliffe.org

To contact the International Bible Society, write

International Bible Society
1820 Jet Stream Dr.
Colorado Springs, CO 80921-3696
Web Site: www.gospelcom.net/ibs
E-Mail: ibs@gospelcom.net

Filling in the Message *extra*

The story of Reuben and his friends from Africa is true. Reuben learned about Jesus from the missionaries, and now he wants to share the good news of Jesus Christ.

Continue to pray that people all around the world and in your backyard may hear the word of God.